FOLIO2

FOLIO 2

THE ELEMENTS OF DESIGN | A publication by **Glen-Gery**

ORO EDITIONS | NOVATO, CALIFORNIA

Welcome to the second edition of *Folio*, a publication devoted to exploring how architectural ideas are made real—to how they are literally materialized in brick.

A publication by Glen-Gery, each issue of *Folio* sets out to unpack the thinking and the design process behind a selection of exceptional buildings to understand how and why a specific material was used.

As with our first issue, the editorial emphasis in the pages that follow is on architectural ideas and, importantly, how those ideas are made real through materials and construction. Thanks to the carefully curated selection of drawings, along with interviews with the projects' architects, *Folio 2* is a source of inspiration and an invaluable reference tool for architects and designers alike.

MARK ELLENOR

PRESIDENT OF GLEN-GERY/BRICKWORKS NORTH AMERICA

Glen-Gery Corporation, part of Brickworks Limited of Australia, is a premier brick and stone manufacturer offering the most diverse product portfolio of more than 600 brick and stone products. For more than a century, Glen-Gery has provided high-quality building products that meet both innovative design challenges and demanding construction specifications. Through technology advancements and product innovations, Glen-Gery delivers a premium product line that caters to the high-style needs of today's architects, designers, and homeowners. Founded in 1890, Glen-Gery is headquartered in Wyomissing, PA. www.glengery.com

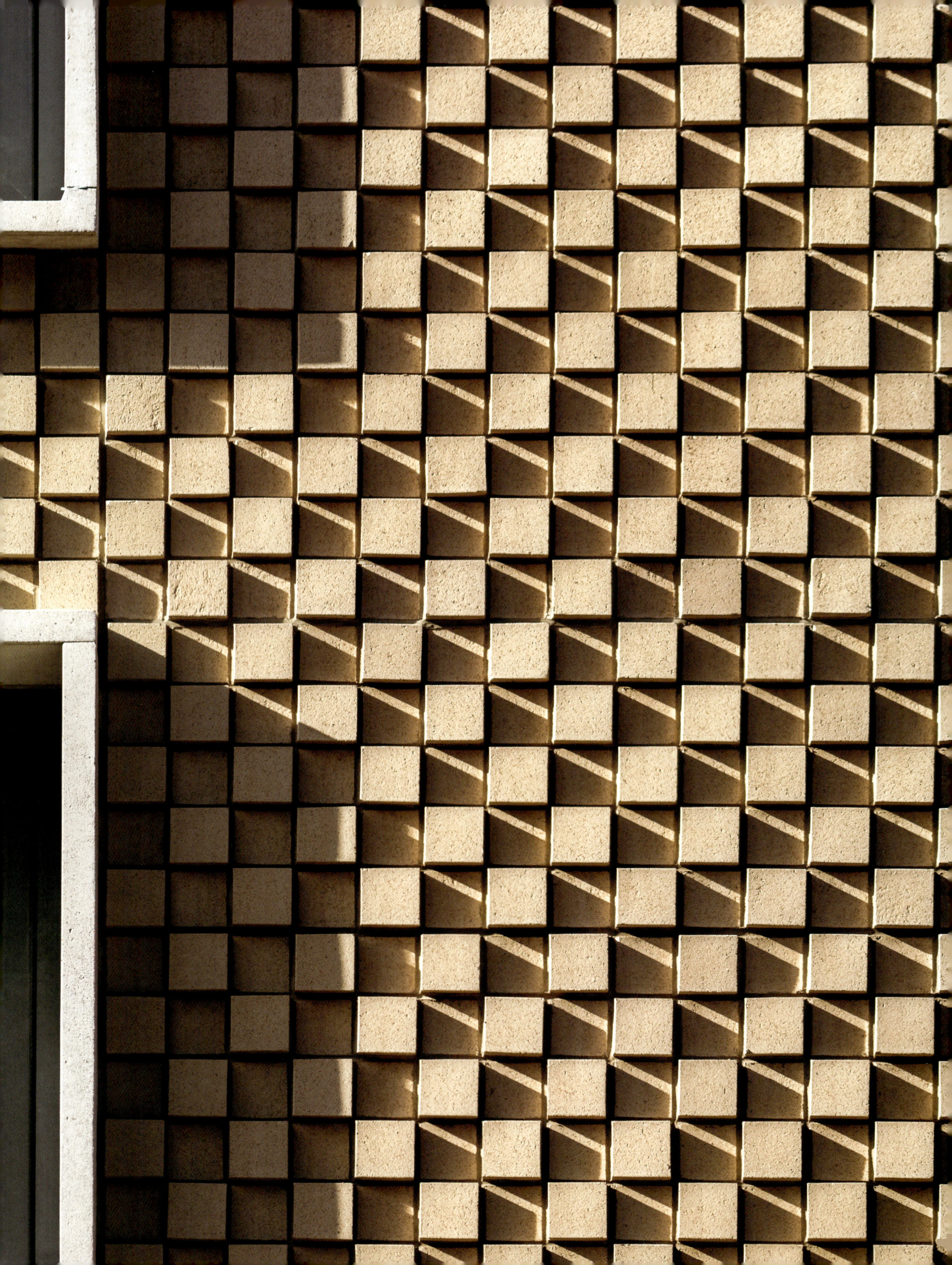

MORRIS ADJMI ARCHITECTS

"If you give me a blank site in the middle of nowhere," says Morris Adjmi, "I don't know where to start." Grounded in history and wedded to their urban context, buildings designed by Morris Adjmi Architects (MA) have a story behind them. At the same time, Adjmi says, MA tries "to find a way to create a relevant architectural statement that isn't mimicking or copying too literally the context." MA looks to bring a newness—without an aggressiveness—to each project, as shown in the three case studies that follow.

Adjmi grew up in New Orleans. "I blame New Orleans for being a beautiful city that attracted me to architecture," he says, "and really focusing on buildings that fit into a bigger picture and don't necessarily scream, hey, look at me." He founded MA in New York in 1997, after working for thirteen years with Pritzker Prize–winning architect Aldo Rossi. The firm worked exclusively in the New York City area during its early years but has more recently designed buildings across the US and into Canada. MA has grown to eighty staff members, and its projects include residential, commercial, and hospitality architecture and interiors.

MA builds in many materials, and brick is a frequent choice. "I do like the flexibility of brick," says Adjmi. "I like the humanity of it, the scale of it, the fact that you can use it in hundreds of different ways, whether it's in the texture or the color or the pattern." He notes the long and continuing history of brick. "Brick is a universal material. It started with mud and then became processed by hand, and then became mechanized and automated in terms of the production." And he recognizes its contemporary possibilities. "I think that it's going through a transformation now in terms of the way it can be applied. It can be panelized, it can be hand laid, and we even see robots assembling bricks."

"Brick is so flexible, but it's also so simple." Adjmi says, "and I think that that's what's really beautiful to me." He continues, "It's almost like there's the brick-and-mortar pixel. It can be taken and manipulated in so many different ways that the possibilities are endless. I never get bored with brick."

THE GRAND MULBERRY

NEW YORK, NEW YORK
UNITED STATES

MOLDED COLLECTION | 56-DD, SPECIAL SHAPES

The brick detailing of The Grand Mulberry—with tripartite banding at base, pediment windows in the middle, and arched windows at top—reference historic Italianate tenements. This seems an almost obvious choice for a new building on Mulberry Street, the last surviving remnant of Little Italy in Manhattan. Yet the detailing is anything but obvious. As Joanne Kaufman wrote in the *New York Times*, the brick pattern "could have emerged from a dot-matrix printer."

Adjmi explains the unique device that MA used on The Grand Mulberry. "The detail on the window surrounds, the coursing of the bricks, the cornice—all of the articulation that you'd normally see in colored brick on these buildings," he says, "we reimagined using dots on the bricks in a series of patterns." The dots are in fact domes built into custom brick. These bricks come in roughly thirty different shapes: double brick with double domes (the most prevalent), double brick with single dome, curved brick, lipped brick, simple shapes without domes, etc. All have a uniform, clay color, and all are laid using a double-stacked running bond coursing. Only the dots are unusual.

"The articulation that you'd normally see in colored brick we reimagined using dots on the bricks in a series of patterns."

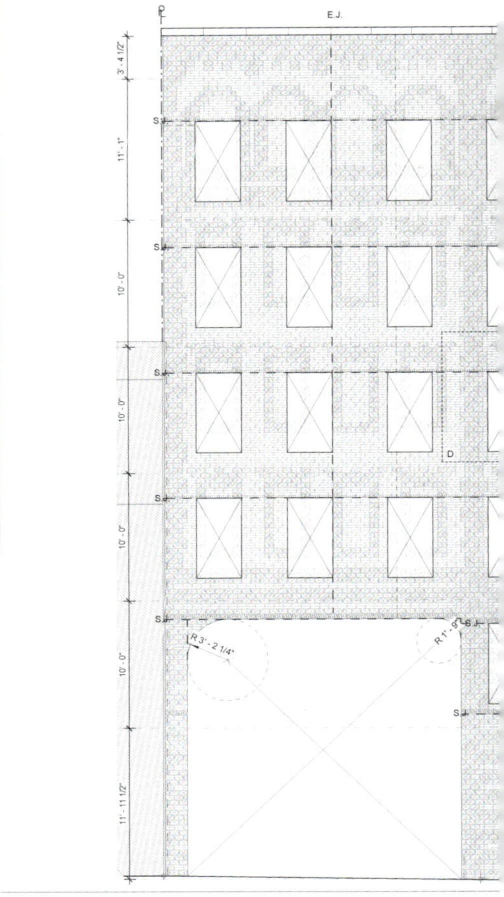

The dotted patterns run on a system separate from that of the new building. "The pattern is an abstraction of a literal copy, as complicated as that sounds," says Adjmi. "The idea was to create something that had the appearance of a historic building." He notes that the classically inspired, irregular grouping of the ghost windows creates a tension or juxtaposition with the regular cadence of real windows. Rows of twelve brick windows meet nine glass windows on the Mulberry Street front, while ten brick windows and eight glass windows are on the Grand Street facade. "It's maybe a little bit of cheating," Adjmi admits, "because we could have done anything we wanted."

TR
Left to right: Mulberry Street, corner, and Grand Street elevations

—

BR
Brick detailing references historic Italianate tenements

L
New building, center, amid brick neighbors in Little Italy

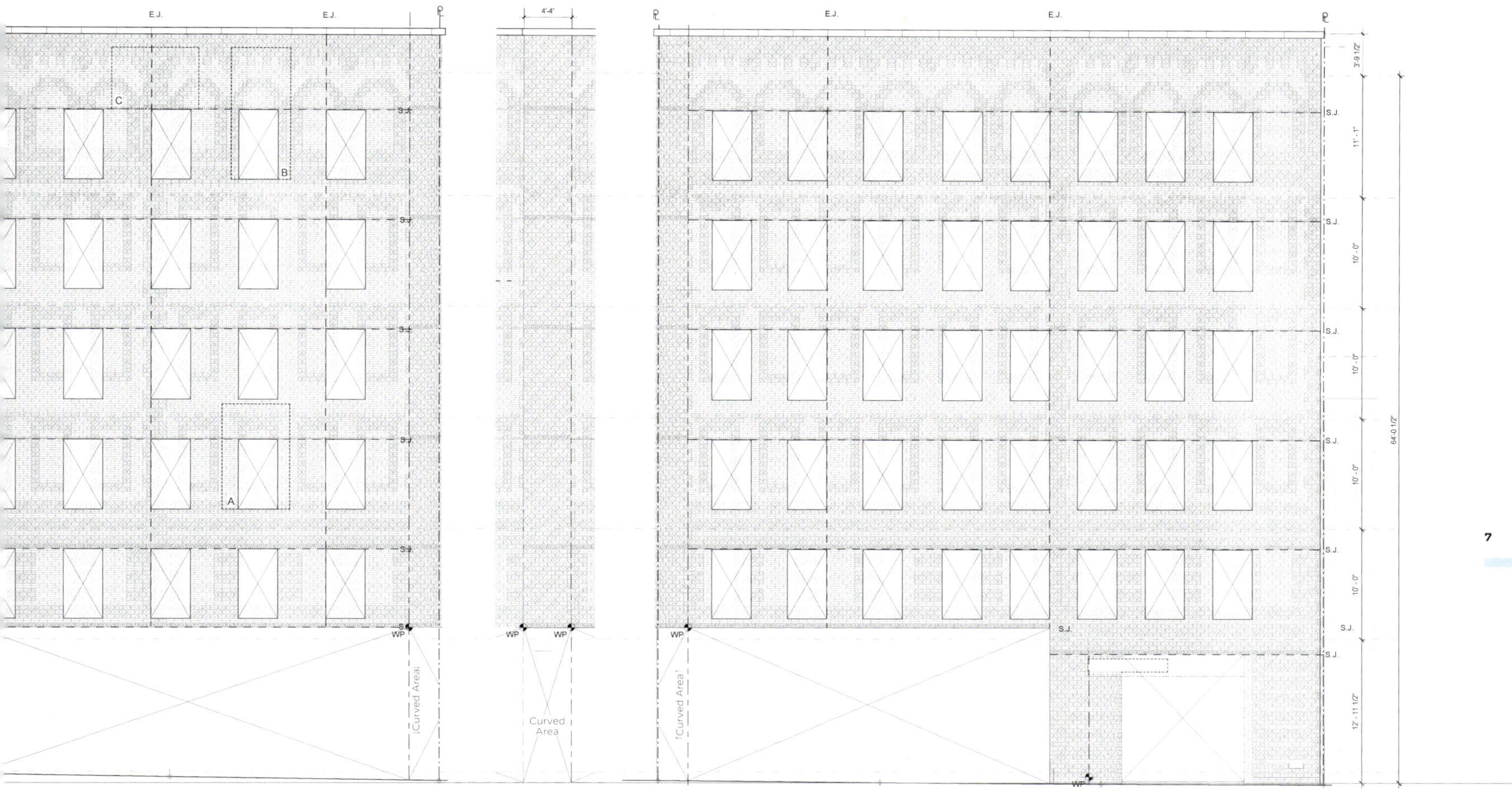
E.J.
E.J.
4'-4"
E.J.
E.J.
S.J.
WP
Curved Area
3'-9 1/2"
11'-1"
10'-0"
10'-0"
10'-0"
10'-0"
12'-11 1/2"
64'-0 1/2"

L
Domes cast into custom bricks allow for patterning on facades

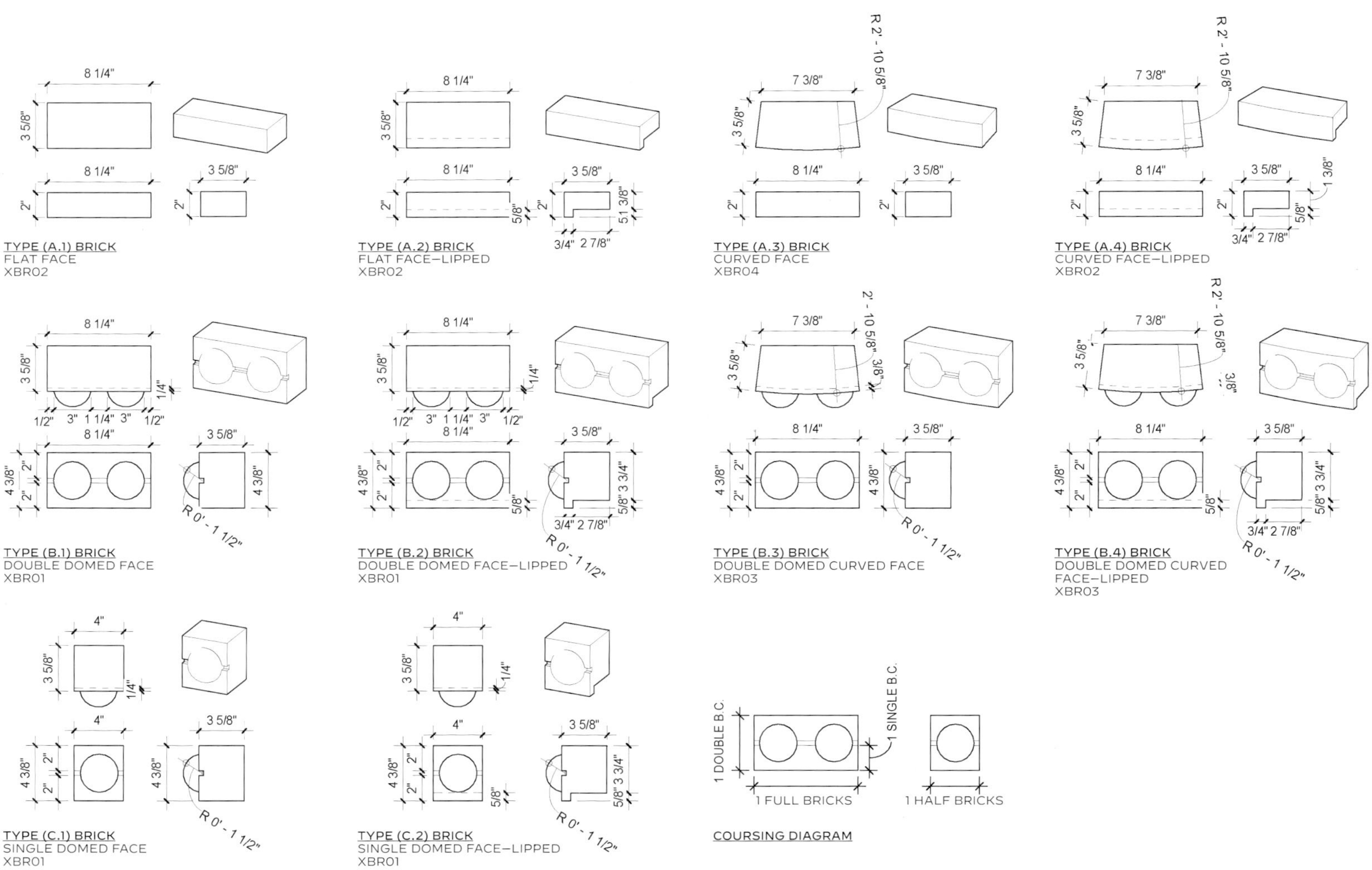

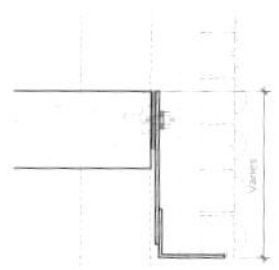

Lintel Elevation Diagram

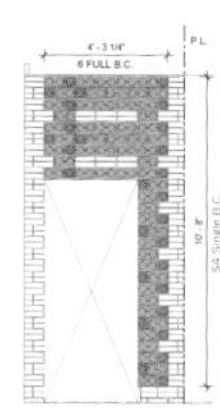

Residential Entry—East Elevation

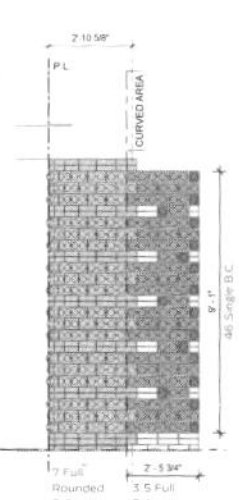

Residential Entry—West Elevation

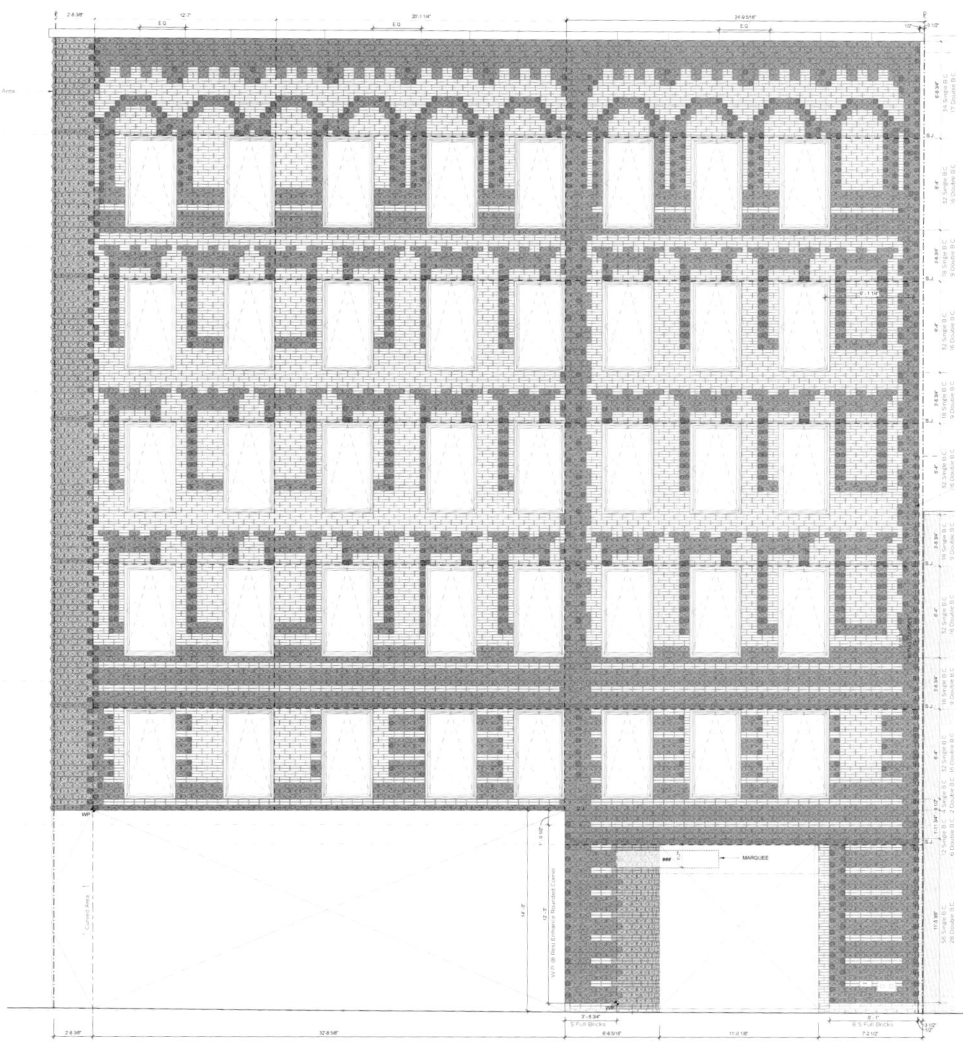

North Elevation

Behind these brick fronts is a seven-story, 35,765 square-foot building with twenty units of housing. The Grand Mulberry is also the new home of the Italian American Museum, which is accessed via a double-height atrium on the ground floor. Adjmi describes the residential interiors as, "warm, minimal, and beautiful." He says, "What we tried to do with the facade, obviously, was to relate to the neighborhood, but also to contrast with the crispness of the modern building inside."

L

Dotted patterns run on system separate from that of new building

—

R

Elevation of Grand Street facade

45 EAST 7TH

NEW YORK, NEW YORK
UNITED STATES

VOGUE COMMERCIAL COLLECTION | DOLOMITE GREY WIRECUT, SPECIAL SHAPES

"I used to think New York was a red brick city, and it is in many places, but if you look at the neighborhood, you see a lot more of that lighter brick."

"I used to think New York was a red brick city, and it is in many places," says Adjmi. "But if you look at the neighborhood around 45 East 7th Street, or the Lower East Side in general, you see a lot more of that lighter brick." He notes the influence of the white buildings at the 1893 Chicago World's Fair in the whitening of Manhattan. "A lot of the architects who were in Chicago were either New York architects or they were Chicago architects who came back to New York." And he points to the white buildings of the Ladies' Mile, a Manhattan shopping district popularized in the late nineteenth century, as an example of their work and influence on the city.

MA uses a light-toned brick in the 34,000-square-foot, seven-story, twenty-one-unit 45 East 7th to reflect the tenement buildings in its locale. Responding to the neighborhood was a necessity, as the site is within the East Village/Lower East Side Historic District and so had to reply to certain codes. But it was also a matter of sensitivity, as the building replaces tenements lost in a 2015 gas explosion. A plaque on 45 East 7th commemorates the two people who died in the event.

The bricks define familiar tripartite facades in a new way. "This building uses brick in a very different way than The Grand Mulberry," says Adjmi. "It is an abstraction, but it's a very literal application in that we created a modern version of some of the buildings that you see in the historic district by using different patterns of brick." The ground level has brick piers in a single corbel pattern. The middle portion sets a custom L-shaped brick in a checkerboard pattern, which was often used below windows or in banding courses on neighborhood buildings. The frieze at the top of 45 East 7th uses a brick pattern with a double corbel.

Adjmi does not seem to be overly concerned that this light, now pristine, surface will weather over time. He talks about the authenticity of materials. "You think about cars—old Jaguars had a waxed-wood dashboard, and now they're dipped in acrylic or Lucite or something, and there's wood back there, but does it really matter? It doesn't smell like wood. It doesn't really look or feel like wood." He continues, "Coming back to bricks, they're real, they get dirty, they get dusty, and they get better with age."

L
Light-toned brick reflects neighbors in Manhattan's Lower East Side

—

B
Brick in single corbel at base, in checkerboard at middle, and in double corbel at frieze

—

R
Timeless materials are used on interior as well

FRONT & YORK

BROOKLYN, NEW YORK
UNITED STATES

VOGUE COMMERCIAL COLLECTION | BELGIAN GREY WIRECUT AND SILVER CITY WIRECUT

"We created the massing in a way that was more like that of late nineteenth-century or early twentieth-century buildings as opposed to what you see more typically now, which is a podium base and the building on top."

At 22 stories, 728 units, and 1,200,000 square feet, Front & York is massive. "It's an enormous project," says Adjmi. "It's a full city block." The collection of services is like a city in itself. "It has eight or nine amenity spaces, a whiskey bar, a wine bar, a kids' playroom, a recording studio, covered outdoor spaces for watching a movie or enjoying a blaze in the fire pit, two pools, a huge fitness center," Adjmi says, "and the subcellar has a basketball court and another pool and all kinds of stuff." MA took on the complex program by breaking it down into various increments—from its overall massing down to its individual bricks.

Adjmi describes Front & York's massing in simple terms: "It's like a rectilinear donut with two towers on opposing corners." The towers hold condominiums, while the lower volumes house rental units. And the donut hole is a park the size of a football field. Michael Van Valkenburgh Associates designed this park as well as the landscaping around the building. That surround is a large amount of space; the building is pulled eighteen feet from the property line. "The wide sidewalks allowed us to create the massing in a way that was more like that of late nineteenth-century or early twentieth-century buildings," says Adjmi, "as opposed to what you see more typically now, which is a podium base and the building on top."

In this and other ways, Front & York follows the model of old warehouse buildings in its neighborhood, Brooklyn's booming DUMBO (Down Under the Manhattan Bridge Overpass). The building's glass fiber reinforced concrete (GFRC) frame with brick infill is a common type among nearby warehouses. MA uses the frame as part of a grid. (Adjmi is fond of grids. The title of his recent monograph is *A Grid and a Conversation*.) "The grid allows the building to read," says Adjmi. "First of all it breaks the building down, but it also makes it more visible from a distance." Front & York has grids within grids: the GFRC introduces the frame, a recessed brick pattern around the windows offers another, and mullions on the window glass supply a third. "These grids are overlaid on each other," says Adjmi, "and I think work from up close as well as far away."

L
Facade has grids within grids: GFRC frame, recessed brick pattern, and window mullions

MA uses standard brick for the project, and it chose Belgian Grey Wirecut and Silver City Wirecut. "We really wanted a silver-grey color, a light color, because of the size of the building and also, we felt, it worked really well with the GFRC," says Adjmi. "For the texture, we wanted to pick something that had enough movement that it didn't appear to be too flat." In this way, the brick is a small but important increment in a substantial design.

TR
View from building to Manhattan Bridge and downtown

—

BR
Massing sketch

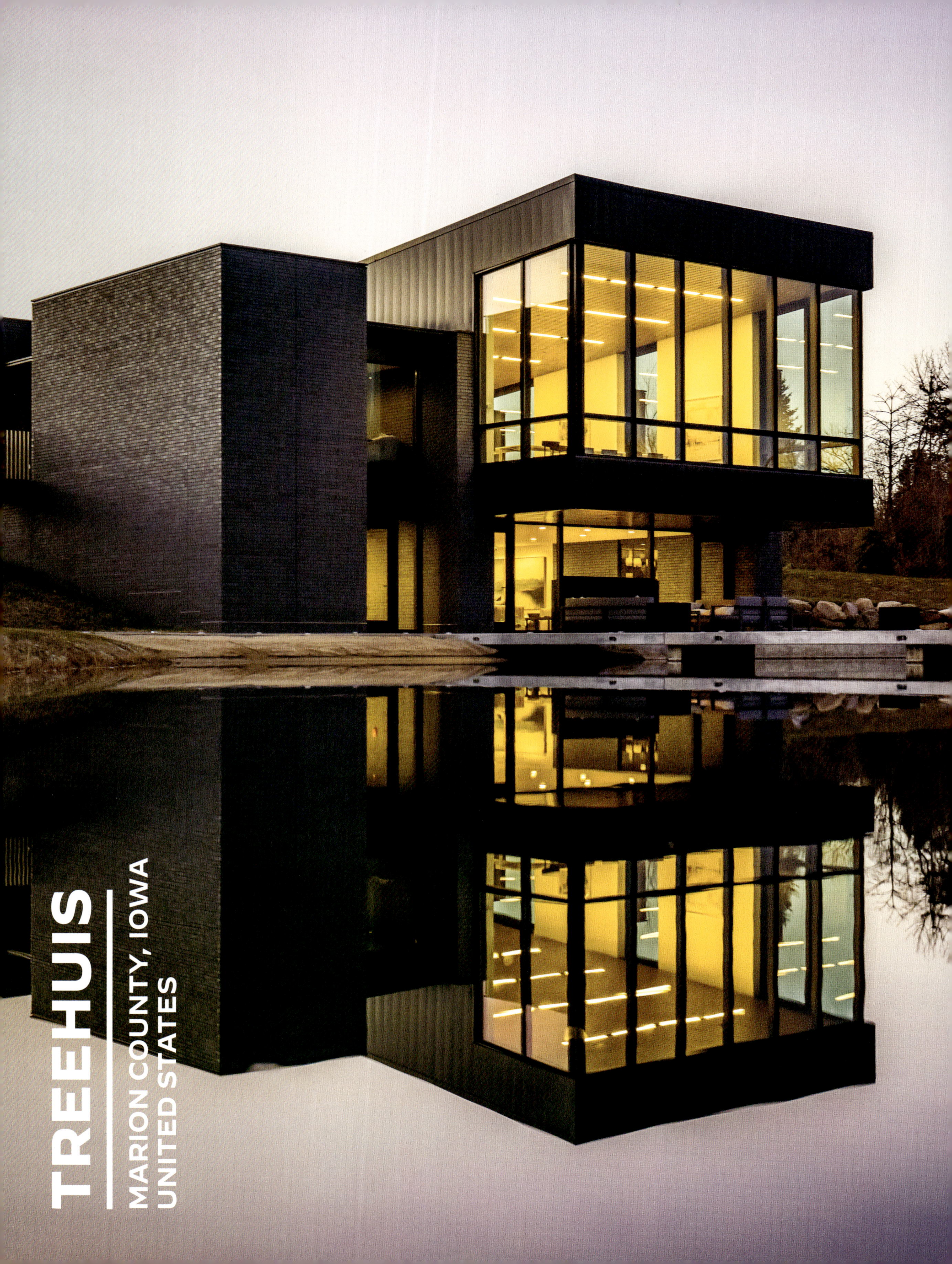

TREEHUIS

MARION COUNTY, IOWA
UNITED STATES

SUBSTANCE ARCHITECTURE

"The dark color of that brick—that's what the dirt looks like here."

As Substance Architecture puts it, Treehuis sits in a hill rather than on a hill. The 7,000-square-foot conference center is a long and low rectangle, with a ground-level green roof instead of a traditional entry facade on its short end. The outstretched sides of the building slowly make their way from the ground to a two-story glass facade at the far end. These sides, uninterrupted walls made of long bricks with barely tooled vertical joints and heavily raked horizontal joints, further emphasize the building's attachment to the ground.

"The dark color of that brick—that's what the dirt looks like here." says Paul Mankins, principal of Substance Architecture. "If you're in Oklahoma, the dirt's red. But if you're in Iowa, dirt is black. It's because the whole state used to be covered with a prairie. Basically, we live in a world that's covered with eight feet of potting soil." The architects chose Ebonite Velour Norman, a brick manufactured in Iowa, to reflect that color. "It emphasizes the fact that the building grows out of the ground a little bit more than, say, a red brick would, or even a brown brick," says Mankins.

The ground is an appropriate focus of the design, as Treehuis sits within a sixty-five-acre picturesque terrain. "The site is actually a former Christmas tree farm," says Mankins. "So you're looking out at this timber landscape." Treehuis, named for this timber, is planned around its idyllic views. The long entry axis leads to a dock over a pond, while a short entry axis arrives at a large conference/dining room with windows onto the landscape.

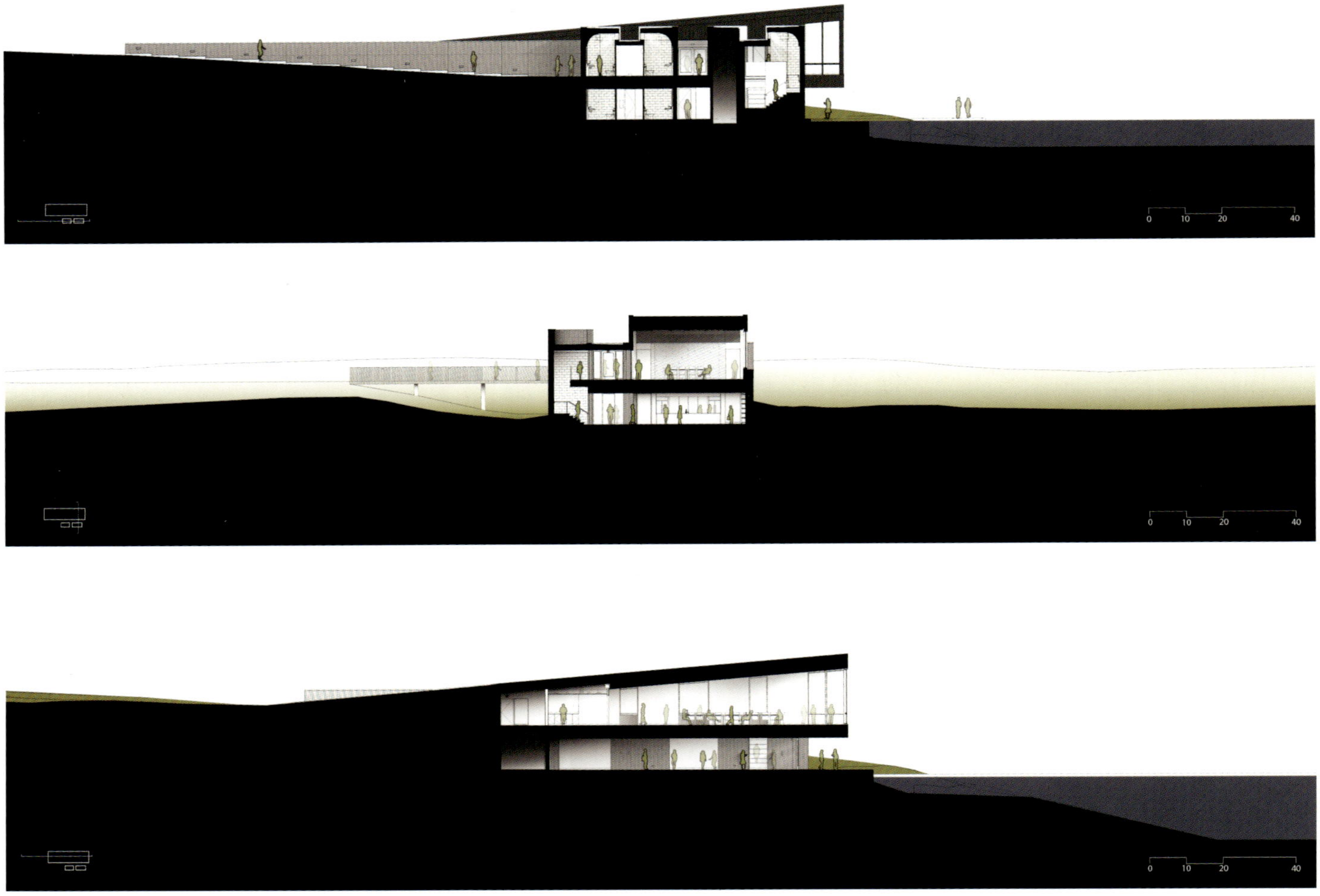

In section, the design responds to Treehuis's site with a high-ceilinged upper floor and a more intimately scaled lower floor. "The upstairs is more about the prospect and being able to take in the view," says Mankins. "The lower level is much more connected—you're right down at the pond level, and you have an outdoor patio condition." The section also reflects the project's unusual program as both a conference center for a family-owned, Marion County–based manufacturing company and a gathering place for that family. The upper floor centers on the large conference room (which doubles as a dining room when the family is using Treehuis), and the lower floor includes a living room, playroom, and ancillary spaces. "The scale of the things, the finishes, the furniture selection," says Mankins, "everything about the lower floor seems much more residential."

The client presented these uncommon requirements to Substance Architecture as a pragmatic list of needs. But Mankins learned that the family's emotional connection to the place was also important to the project. As some members of the multigenerational, extended family had separated from the company and moved away from Marion County—a not uncommon thing in any large family—it was looking for a way to keep ties to the place. "They want their kids to think, oh, my memories of this town are it's this fun place that I went with my cousins, and we got to do water sports in the pond, and we got to shoot skeet out in the back forest, and we got to go hiking," says Mankins. "That's really what this is for—to reconnect the family to the company and to connect them to themselves."

L
Sections show building sits in hill rather than on hill

R
Upper floor takes in view while lower level is connected to pond

TR
Upper floor centers on large conference room, which doubles as dining room

—

BR
Lower floor includes living room, playroom, and ancillary spaces

Mankins suspects that the company's chair had an additional audience in mind for the building. "I think that part of the attraction for him, Mankins says, "was trying to communicate that the company had a forward-looking mindset." Treehuis's contemporary aesthetic—its earthbound, green-roofed, brick-clad form—might just help attract design and engineering talent to Marion County.

L
Using one brick, building achieves material continuity from inside to outside

MORGAN PARC

MINEOLA, NEW YORK
UNITED STATES

STEPHEN B. JACOBS GROUP

When the developer of Morgan Parc requested a "timeless" design for a new residential complex in Long Island's Mineola, the Stephen B. Jacobs Group (SBJ) turned to a familiar model. The architects took inspiration from late-nineteenth- and early-twentieth-century mill buildings common to the Northeast (if not to Mineola). "Those buildings were made in order to allow a lot of light in the factories," says SBJ associate Gavri Slasky, "but they also provide for beautiful living spaces with floor-to-ceiling glass." SBJ had experience in reworking precedents for new uses. "My boss, Stephen Jacobs [founder of SBJ], would tell us stories of the work that our firm did back in the 1970s," says Slasky. "A lot of it was adaptive reuse—taking commercial buildings and converting them to residential lofts. I'm sure that was in the back of his head."

SBJ borrowed not only the mill building type for Morgan Parc, but also the mill's traditional material: brick. "We wanted to make one, unified building with one material," says Slasky, "whereas you would see a lot of other architects and developers breaking up the mass of the building by using different materials." With this in mind, SBJ looked to add variety to the brick facades. It first considered using a blend of bricks, with a few different shades of each. "We went through many different selections until we came to the Glen-Gery brick," says Slasky. "One thing that we really loved about this brick was that it had so much variation, even within its single source." He continues, "It's the process of how the brick is made in the kiln that provides for the variation. But it's all the same base brick."

"We wanted to make one, unified building with one material."

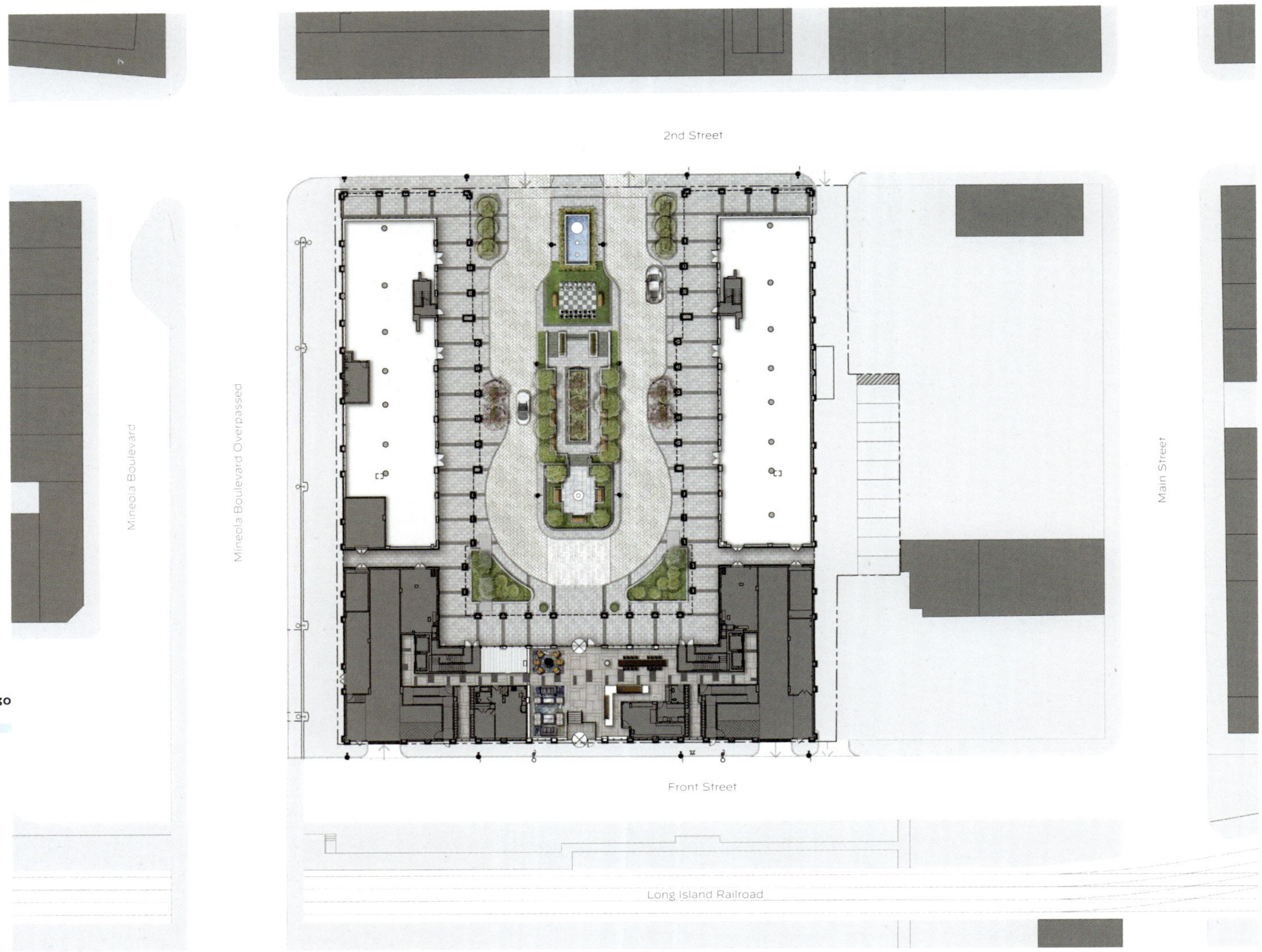

Variety also comes to Morgan Parc in the brick's detailing. This includes projections, recessions, corbeling, and checkerboard patterns. "We also had a unique shape that we created," says Slasky, "which was this curved brick that's part of our piers." SBJ collaborated with local masons to work out the intricacies of these details. "We walked the scaffolding together, taking a look at things that we liked, things that we didn't like," says Slasky. "It was really about perfecting three or four different details. Once they had that, they were able to run with it throughout the building."

To add even more variety to the 317,000-square-foot project, SBJ broke the large mass into sections. Morgan Parc's one- and two-bedroom apartments and ground-floor retail form a U around a courtyard. The back of the U faces railroad tracks, frequented by Mineolan workers commuting into New York City. The building is tallest at this end of the site, where other tall buildings are located. The volume steps down from this height to a lower scale at 2nd Street, which is part of the town's historic center.

L
Plan showing back of U facing railroad tracks and sides opening to 2nd Street

—

R
Projections, recessions, corbeling, and checkerboard patterns add variety to brick facade

TL
North elevation

—

BL
Courtyard—with plantings, benches, water feature, and car drop-off—is open to public

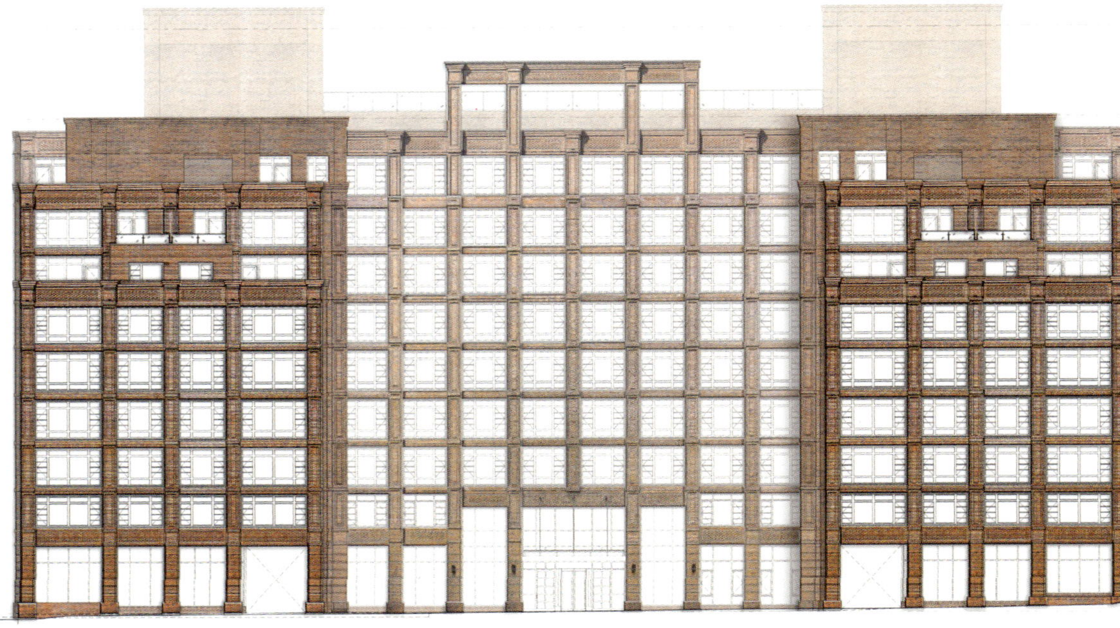

R

Courtyard elevation

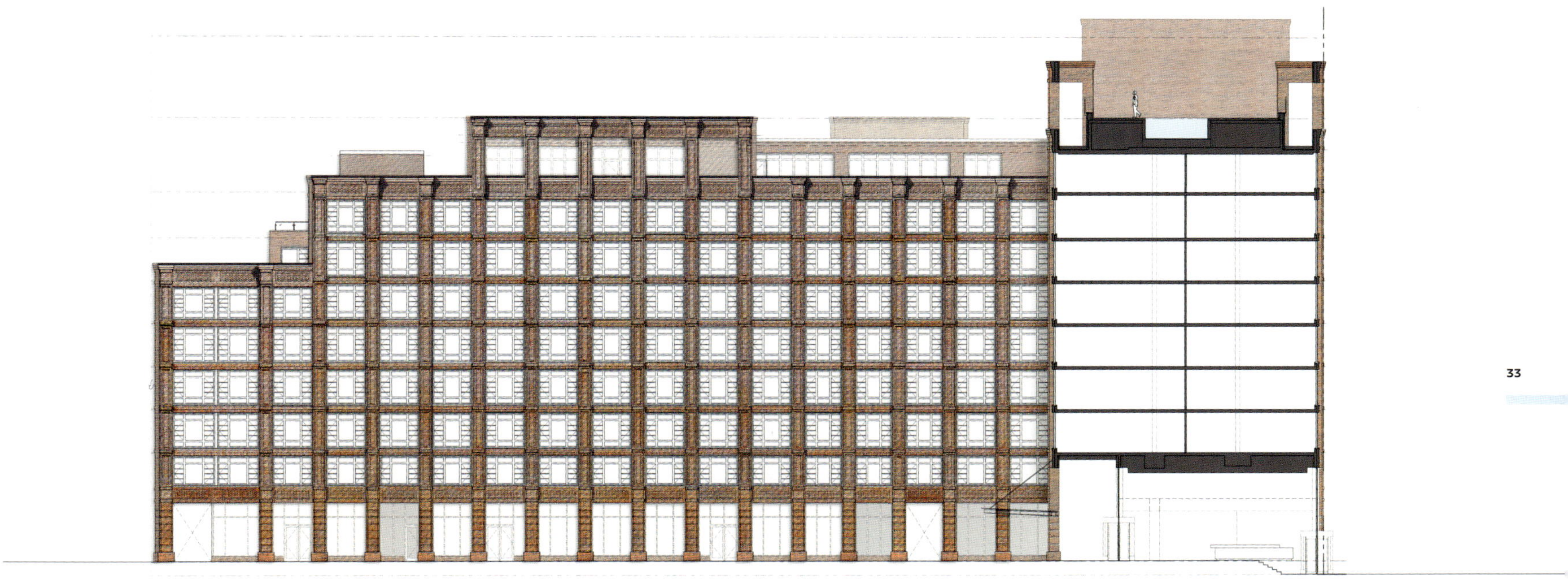

Morgan Parc's courtyard is open to the public, not just to renters of its one- and two-bedroom apartments or users of its ground-floor retail. The formally designed space—with plantings, benches, a water feature, and a car drop-off—is the site of Mineola's annual tree lighting ceremony. "We were always thinking about how to integrate the town into our building," says Slasky, "and our building into the town."

Slasky notes some favorable reception to SBJ's traditional design. "I've taken people to this building, and they've asked me, 'Oh, what was this building before?'" he says. "I took that as a compliment, even though at heart I'm a modernist and I love to make new buildings. But I really appreciated that people thought that this had a life beforehand."

L
View from lounge
to sky level
pool deck

TR
Apartment dining area and kitchen

—

BR
Seating area of residential lobby

RANSOM DISTRICT LIBRARY

PLAINWELL, MICHIGAN
UNITED STATES

TOWER PINKSTER

"The building changes throughout the day, because some of the brick absorbs light, some of it reflects light, and then sometimes it looks like just one brick, so that's kind of fun."

At the entrance facade of the Ransom District Library, visitors come upon one of many connections between the building and the sun. Here powder-coated aluminum lines radiate from a projecting rod, referencing a sundial that formerly occupied the site. "It's kind of abstract," says Tony Reiner, senior architectural designer at TowerPinkster, "but still you'll notice the shadow lines tell a story about time and the equinox and the solstice." The light metal of the sculpture contrasts the brick surface of the wall behind it. "The brick does a really nice job, I think, of highlighting that shadow," says Reiner.

TowerPinkster used two slightly different bricks on the 20,000-square-foot library. "One of the bricks is smooth and one is a velour, so we're going back to the story of the sunlight," says Reiner. "The building changes throughout the day, because some of the brick absorbs light, some of it reflects light, and then sometimes it looks like just one brick, so that's kind of fun."

Choosing brick for the Ransom District Library was not surprising. The project is in Plainwell, a two-square-acre, southwestern Michigan city where most of the downtown storefronts are brick. Plainwell was settled in the 1830s around a paper mill, and the designers found inspiration in the raw steel bridges—specifically the dark color of the bridges—that used to extend from the mill. "The texture of the city informs the material, and then the nature of this industry informs the color," says Reiner. "In a way, that lets the library be a signature piece for the community, because there's not another dark brick building here."

Ransom District Library is sited on the east bank of the Kalamazoo River. In working with the library director and associate library director on the scheme, TowerPinkster determined that a strictly orthogonal approach would not do. "They said, well, the river is fluid, and the building has a bit of a language that ties into something fluid," says Reiner. "That's when some of these softer curves started coming in as a subtle way to tie into that movement." These curves can be seen in the library's perimeter walls, the building massing, and the roof projections.

A larger curve in the library's plan had a more practical origin. "One of the big drivers was they wanted a book drop," says Reiner. "The site was pretty challenging for that, so we took the building and rotated it slightly. And then the eastern facade is a giant curve, so that we could fit in that book drop."

The design also responds to complex programming and space planning. "Libraries are evolving beyond just collections and venues for night events," says Reiner. Ransom District Library reflects how the community wanted to use the space in what TowerPinkster calls a "library of experiences." The stacks are positioned in the building's center and lit by a north-facing clerestory to protect books from the sun's harsh rays. This collection is then ringed by a variety of rooms. "There's the children's room, the teen space, a large community space for meetings and presentations," says Reiner. "And then as you move around to the east you have the city archives." This is followed by a high-tech maker space, staff offices, a café, and small study rooms. "These are all soundproofed," says Reiner, "so you can take drum sets in there, you can jam on a guitar, you can study, and it won't disrupt anyone in the stacks." There is also a dedicated performance space that opens onto an outdoor deck.

L
Dark brick sets library apart from other local brick buildings

"And then the showstopper," says Reiner, "is that element on the west—the reading room." Its floor-to-ceiling glass walls, a marked change from the brick-clad walls of the library's other three facades, open west to a view of the Kalamazoo. Here the sunlight can pour in, and the sunset can be enjoyed.

TR
South and east elevations

—

BR
Brick curves share fluidity of adjacent Kalamazoo River

L

Radiating lines at entry reference sundial that formerly occupied site

TR
Plan showing central stacks ringed by ancillary spaces

—

BR
North and west elevations

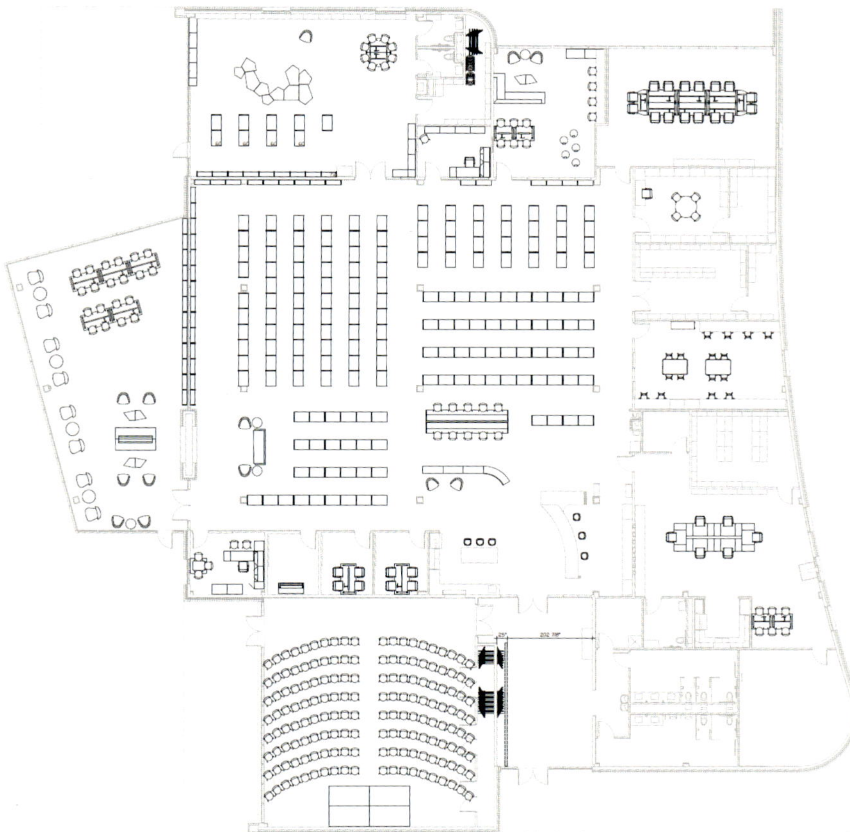

GILFORD COURT

MCLEAN, VIRGINIA
UNITED STATES

PETER VANDERPOEL

"Brick automatically provides you with a rhythm, and it's a module that you work with. Bricks provide their own organization."

In the design of Gilford Court, architect Peter VanderPoel used several organizing systems to manage an expansive program on a steep site. The house is located in a residential enclave on the outskirts of Washington, DC. VanderPoel began by breaking it into three masses—garage, semipublic area, and private spaces—and setting these on three levels. "Think about these three blocks stacked on top of each other, with a hinge at each point—they splay out." These hinges contain stairs between the volumes, with simple steps at the intersection of the garage and semipublic volume and with a commanding, curving staircase between the semipublic and the private blocks.

The turns between the three volumes respond in part to the topography of the site, with the garage at the lowest level and the other two volumes branching up and out. But they also adhere to other, more abstract systems. "This gets esoteric pretty quickly," VanderPoel says, "but it has to do with polyrhythms and geometry."

"Polyrhythm is an overlaying of two rhythms," he explains. "It's common in West Africa. You've got regular rhythms, but they overlap in a way that makes everything more interesting." He continues, "So I've got these three axes on the site. And each mass tends to run on its own axis; but when they intersect, something different happens."

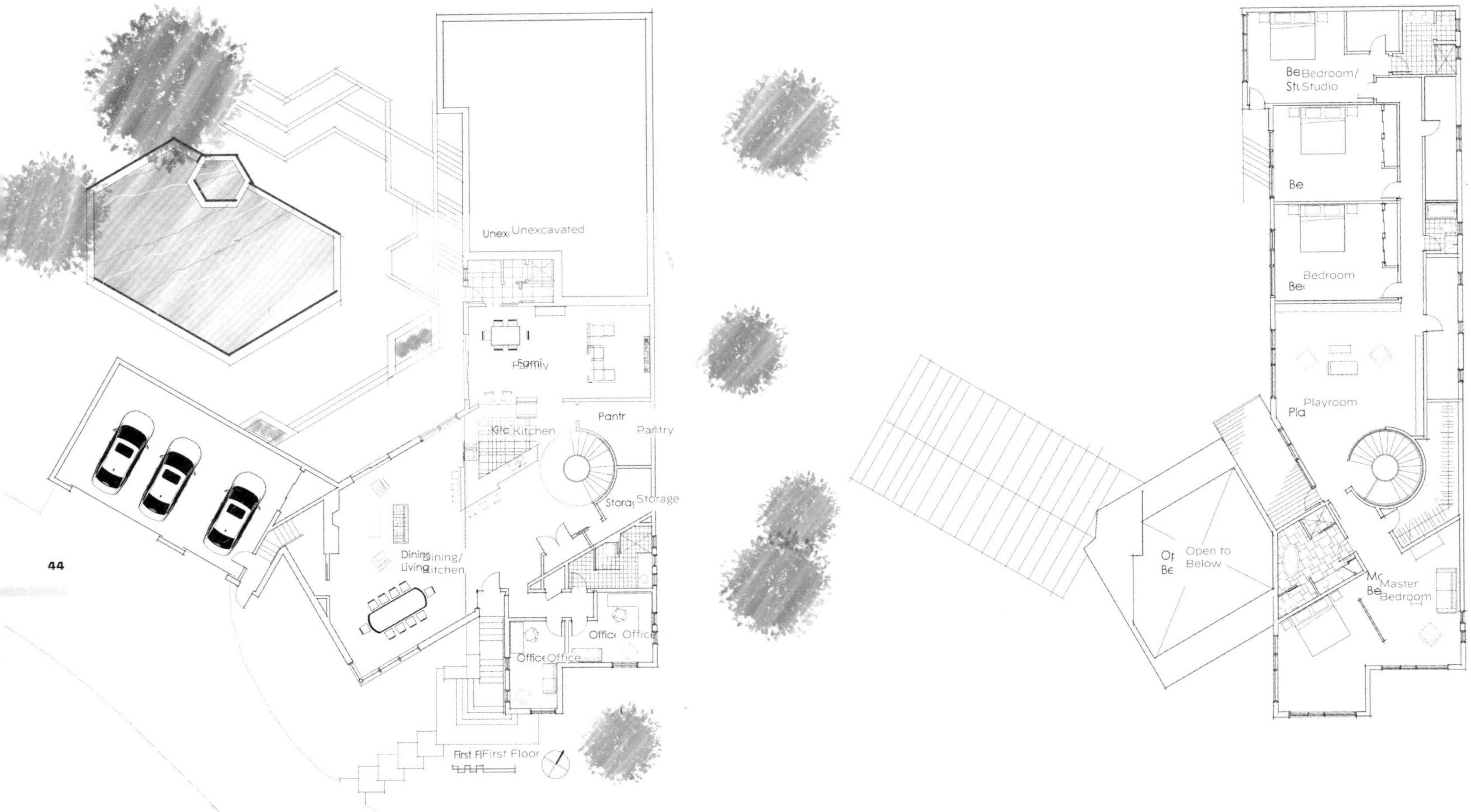

These axes are positioned according to the geometry of a hexagon—that is, at 60-degree angles—which the architect laid as a grid onto the site. The nontraditional grid allowed for multiple opportunities. "I can start to pick up other axes depending on what I need to do in these different blocks," he says. "The other geometries will show up. And because they've already been established, they don't appear out of order."

In this way, polyrhythmic and geometric regulations set the groundwork for Gilford Court. But VanderPoel did not force the two organizing systems onto the site. "I don't think of architecture as an imposition," he says. "It's a discovery that this site has solutions that are embedded into it, having to do with where the sun is, the neighbors, what are the materials, and so on."

VanderPoel used three main materials—brick, carbonized wood, and fiber cement siding—on the exterior of Gilford Court. He planned to use one material for each of the three volumes. The garage would be faced in wood, while the private block would be enclosed in fiber cement siding, a material that allowed for a complex composition of bedroom windows. "The middle block—the semipublic block—had to do with the neighborhood," says VanderPoel. He designed this block in brick to connect to that tradition. "Northern Virginia is all about brick. It's tried and true, and it's durable and doesn't need maintenance."

L
First floor and second floor plans show building volumes splaying from hinges

R
Brick, carbonized wood, and fiber cement siding are used on exterior

L
A nontraditional grid allowed for multiple opportunities

—

R
Wood meets brick in interior

As built, these three materials run into each other—a wall of brick next to a wall of wood on the same volume. This is fine by the architect. "It's part of that whole polyrhythmic sharing," he says. The design change had another benefit. VanderPoel wanted to avoid manufacturing special bricks or laying awkward joints at the 60-degree corners, and meeting brick wall to wood wall helped to keep the corner lines clean.

Of all the regulating systems used at Gilford Court, brick seems to be one of the least complex. "It automatically provides you with a rhythm," VanderPoel's says, "and it's a module that you work with. Bricks provide their own organization."

TR
Spiral stair serves as hinge between semipublic and private areas

—

BR
First floor sauna and shower

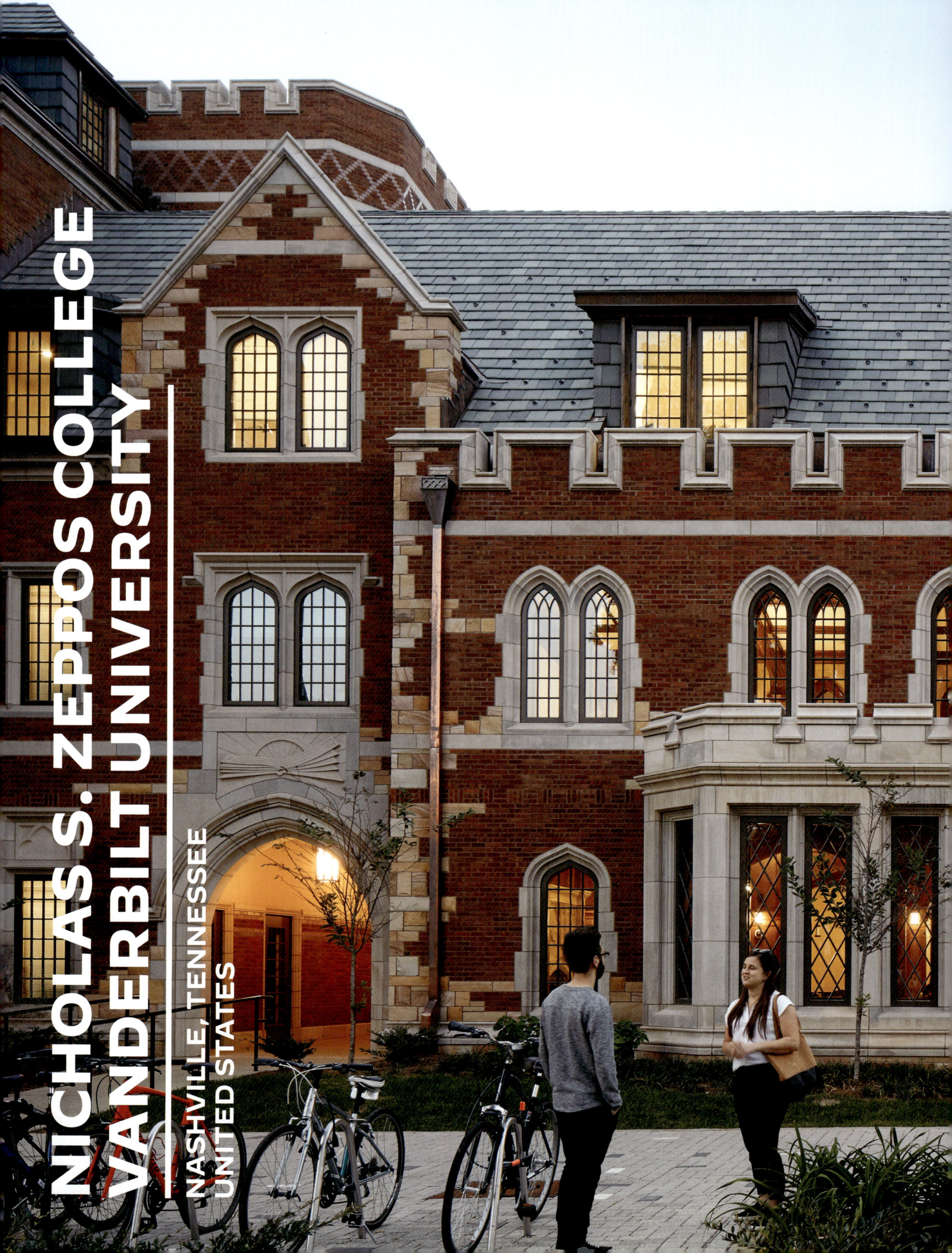

NICHOLAS S. ZEPPOS COLLEGE
VANDERBILT UNIVERSITY

NASHVILLE, TENNESSEE
UNITED STATES

DAVID M. SCHWARZ ARCHITECTS

In designing Nicholas S. Zeppos College, David M. Schwarz Architects (DMSAS) borrowed a traditional type—residential colleges—for twenty-first-century student housing. The residential college model, communities of 300–400 students, "captures this notion of a more holistic, supportive, living-and-learning environment," says Steve Knight, principal of DMSAS. "And it's a bit of 'what's old is new again,' because this is very much in the tradition, going all the way back to Oxford and Cambridge, Yale and Princeton."

Zeppos College is one of four colleges that DMSAS is designing for Vanderbilt University, and these replace four 1960s-era high-rise dormitories. Rather than the tower-in-a-field plan of older dormitories, the new colleges are positioned on opposite sides of Alumni Lawn and linked together by a promenade. "Each one of these is on the order of several hundred thousand square feet," says Knight, "so it was important that the buildings step down to be very humane in scale." DMSAS carefully considered the massings of the residential bars. "We decided that a maximum height would be five stories so that, as the bars were shaped to create courtyards to get natural light to the inside-facing rooms, those courtyards would have a pleasant feeling to them," says Knight. "If the buildings got much taller, those courtyards wouldn't be courtyards anymore. They would be light shafts."

"It's a bit of 'what's old is new again,' because this is very much in the tradition, going all the way back to Oxford and Cambridge, Yale and Princeton."

Each college has distinguishing characteristics that establish its identity for its residents. Zeppos College includes a prominent tower with apartments for visiting faculty and scholars and a conference center at the top. Each college also has a publicly accessible dining room and great room as well as a program-specific magnet element. These are meant to help attract students from other parts of the campus.

BL
Courtyards offer light to inside-facing rooms

—

R
Prominent tower with apartments for visiting faculty and scholars and conference center at top

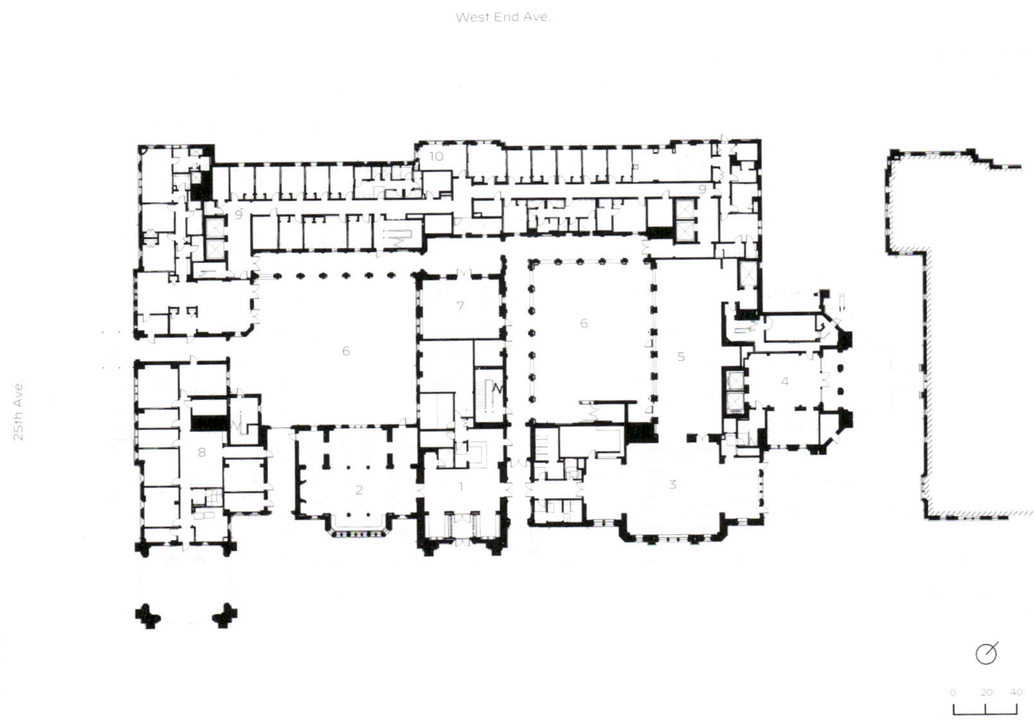

LEVEL 1 FLOOR PLAN

1. Main Lobby
2. Great Room
3. Dining Room
4. Tower Lobby
5. Kitchen
6. Courtyard
7. Shared Living Room
8. Offices
9. Sleeping Quarters
10. Group Music

The design of Zeppos College marries its traditional model to a traditional architectural style. "With the client, we visited a variety of campuses around the States," says Knight, "and everybody concluded that tying to the Collegiate Gothic tradition was the right way to go. So that's, first and foremost, what you're seeing on the exterior." Pointed arches, bay windows, masonry construction, and ornate decoration distinguish the type. "It's very picturesque," says Knight. "It's a very casual style."

TL
Collegiate Gothic tradition influences style of Zeppos College

—

BL
Brick is complemented with Indiana limestone and colorful Crab Orchard stone

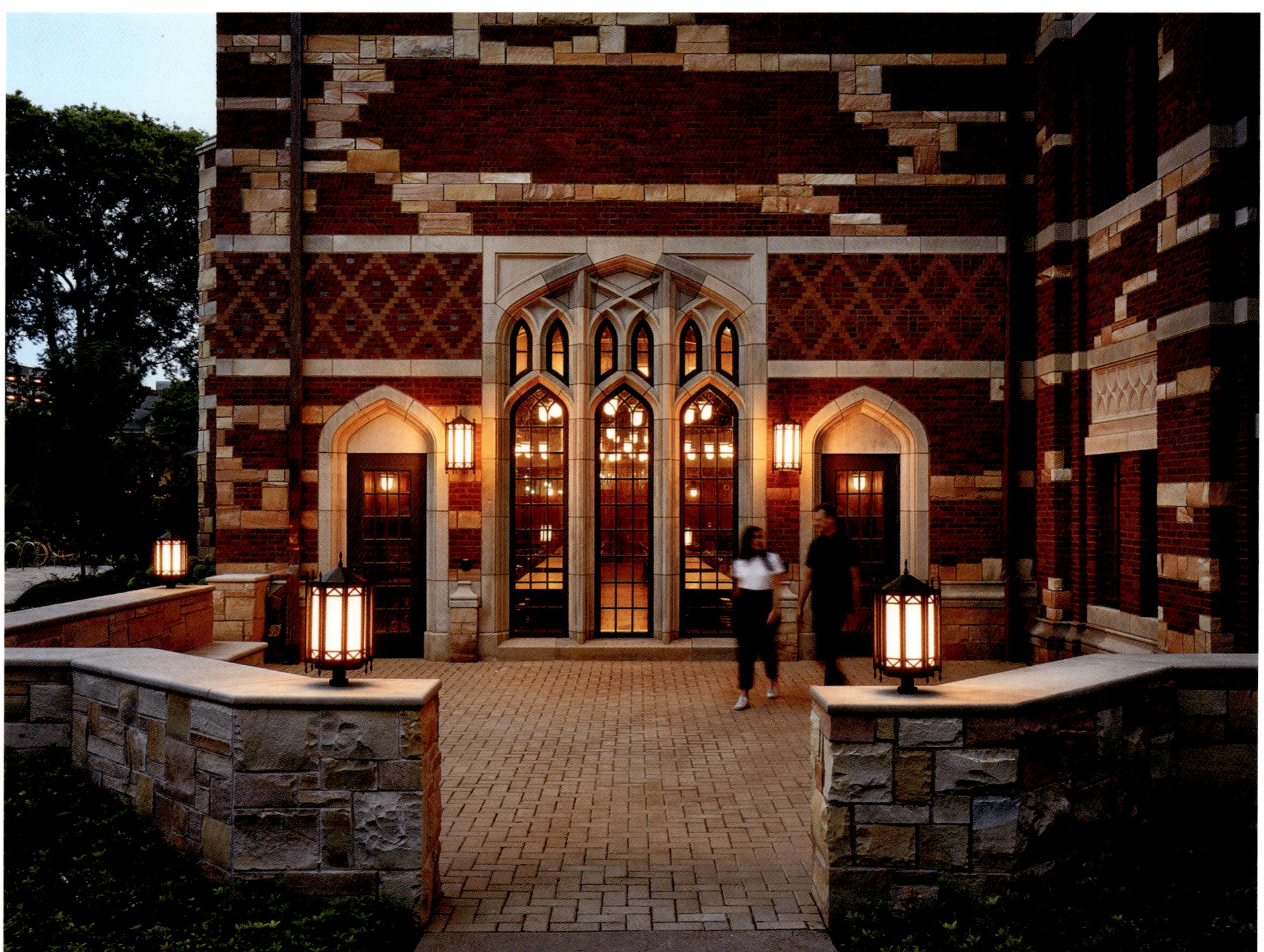

R
Collegiate Gothic motifs continue on interior

The Collegiate Gothic, Knight says, allows for variation in the quartet of residential colleges. "You can tell they're all from the same family, but each one has a slightly different personality." He continues, "If you just put some extra thought in employing architectural expressions, you can eke out a lot of interesting variety so that each building has its own slightly different expression, but yet they all feel very much cut from the same cloth."

Part of this variety is expressed in the four buildings' slightly different coloration, which the architects achieved by tweaking the combinations of brick types on the facades—38% Catawba, 28% 4-HB, and 34% 47-HB for Zeppos. These bricks are complemented with Indiana limestone ("you find it on great public buildings everywhere," Knight says) and colorful Crab Orchard stone from Tennessee, which the architects use as "sprinkle" on the facade. "Another key feature," Knight says, "is this use of what we call 'decorative polychrome,' which is where we've added some additional bricks to the palette to create decorative patterns—for example, a basket weave that was rendered with ironspot bricks."

The materials are combined with what appears to be tricky detailing. "It used to be very common," says Knight. "It's not so much anymore." He credits many people in executing the complex design. "I think this is an incredible team of designers, as well as technicians and builders and craftspeople," says Knight, "who were able to employ modern building techniques and yet still build very durable, long-lasting buildings that look beautiful."

H-HOUSE

MANOTICK, ONTARIO
CANADA

EVERYDAY STUDIO

"The technologies implemented in the house are quite advanced and promote sustainable systems. But the building models of the house itself are quite traditional."

"What I try to achieve with my work is a sense of timelessness," says Mateusz Nowacki, principal of Everyday Studio, "that the house appears minimal in its execution and in its detailing, but it harkens back to very traditional methodologies of building." Nowacki's H-House in Manotick, Ontario exemplifies this approach. It has the limited volumes, clean lines, natural materials, and big, pitched roofs that are true to both contemporary and historical buildings.

The house connects to the history of its locale. Manotick, a community now in the City of Ottawa and a short commute from downtown, was once a farming village. "There's a connection to those agrarian structures by using these A-frame forms," says Nowacki, "that represent a very pure idea of what it means to clad a volume for living with a roof." Though the A-frame type was common in Manotick's older buildings, it has not been popular with H-House's recent neighbors. "The neighborhood is made up of a lot of really large houses that have a very formal appearance," says Nowacki. "And a lot of the sculpting of the architecture of those houses exists within the roof geometry, because they have so many wings and adaptations and additions. The roof geometry ends up being very noisy, visually."

The H form of H-House is meant to quiet the noise, to bring simplicity and purpose to the home's wings and their roofs. The H is derived in part from Nowacki's insistence on cross-ventilation, which he says, can only be achieved when the depth of a volume is limited to roughly thirty-five feet. That narrow increment for this large house became a basis for long and thin volumes, which Nowacki forms into an H. Its two legs are clad in brick, meant to ground the house, and its double-height center bar in standing seam metal, more conceptually appropriate for a floating volume. The H form creates two courtyards, one at the south entrance and one at the north, where it offers respite during hotter summer days.

TL
Wood insertions on brick facade suggest large wooden shutters

—

BL
Diagram illustrating H form of house

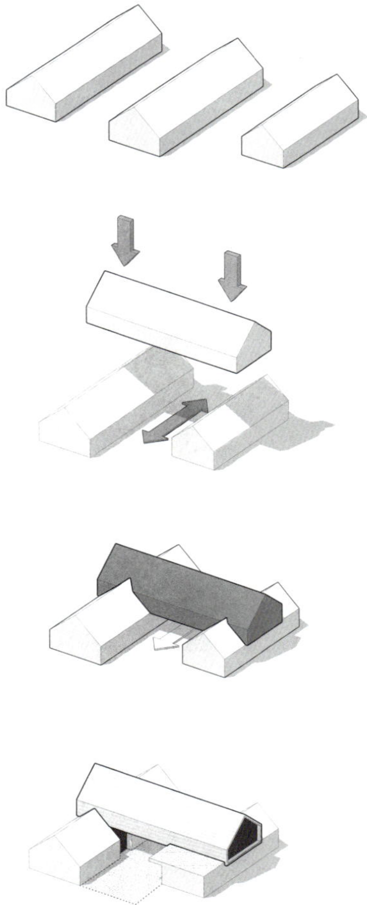

Nowacki used Sioux City Smoked Tudor Velour brick on the project. "The selection of the color and tone of the brick harkened back to how brick was used before we started introducing acid washes and color tones," he says. "In Canada, a lot of the buildings from the late 1800s came out of brick factories in Toronto that primarily produced clay-colored brick." This nostalgic choice sat well with the house's clients, who grew up in small clay-brick-clad villages in Eastern Europe.

The architect liked the color variation among the smokey bricks and how the color reflects the leaves of the maple trees that surround H-House. "The brick was getting installed in the house in early fall, right when the colors started to change," he says. "You could see the effect of the material on the house and that interplay between those colors." He says the brick also sits well in Ottawa's long snow-covered season. "Having a house clad in darker tones and of saturated clay-colored material provides a sense of warmth in the winter."

R
Cantilever at entrance, where brick almost seems to float

H-House plays with this conventional brick in unconventional ways. These include a cantilever at the entrance, where brick almost seems to float. Another contemporary move is allowing the brick to come up to the peak of the A-frame itself, with its load pushed to steel bands at the roof edges. "The technologies implemented in the house are quite advanced and promote sustainable systems," says Nowacki. "But the building models of the house itself are quite traditional."

L
Two legs are clad in brick and double-height center bar in standing seam metal

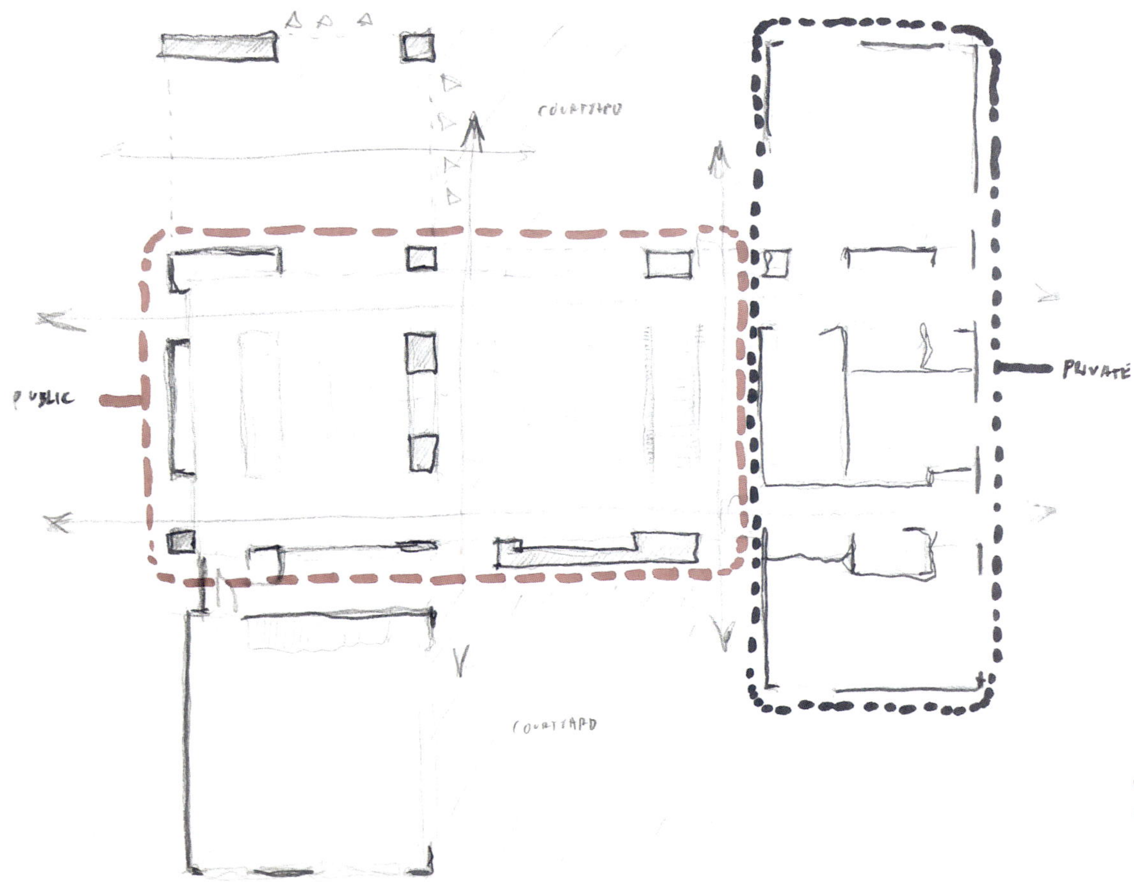

TR
Sketch of plan showing private and public areas

—

BR
Legs at rear frame courtyard

L
Same brick is used on exterior and fireplace

—

TR
Brick color reflects leaves of surrounding maple trees

—

BR
Wall of main kitchen hides pantry and secondary kitchen behind

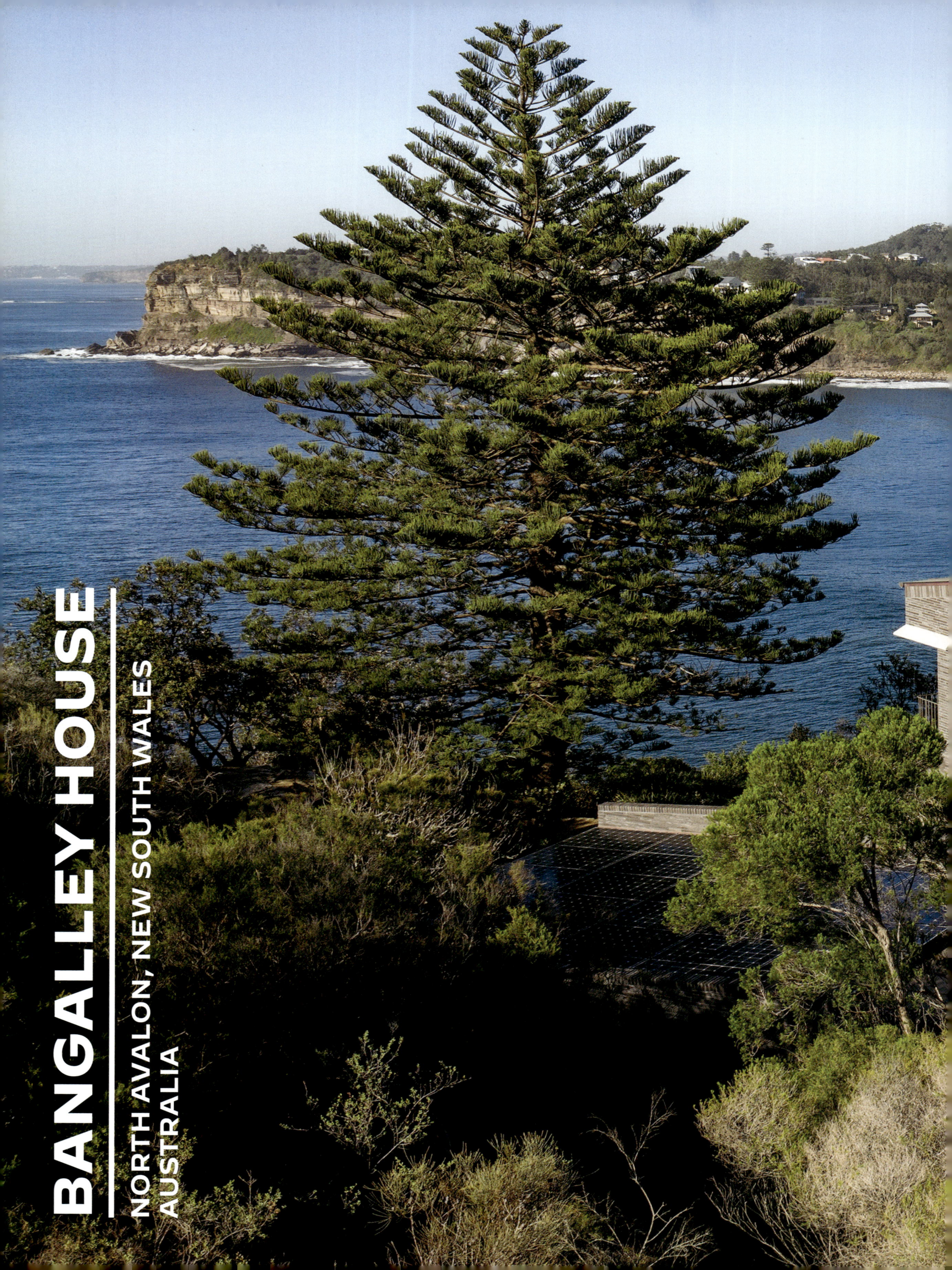

BANGALLEY HOUSE

NORTH AVALON, NEW SOUTH WALES
AUSTRALIA

CASEY BROWN ARCHITECTURE

"It couldn't be a frail construction. It had to be something very substantial."

"Would you believe this is the first brick house in thirty-five years I've ever built?" asks Rob Brown, cofounder of Casey Brown Architecture. "For me it wasn't really a material that I had embraced." His firm, based in East Sydney, is known for its contemporary work built in glass, steel, and timber.

But for Bangalley House, brick was a good choice for its site—a sandstone and shale outcrop overlooking the Pacific Ocean, north of Sydney. "When looking at the headland, the horizontality of the rock face is a very strong feature," says Brown. "What we wanted to do was reflect, without copying, the horizontality with a long, skinny brick." Brown chose long-format San Selmo brick handmade in Venice and in a variety of colors. "I had a selection of six different colors," he says, " and I mixed them up a bit to try to create this diversity that you see in that cliff face."

The brick serves another purpose: it responds to the clients' brief to build a house that would last a hundred years. "Functionally brick is extremely rugged and tough for a location that really faces the Antarctic," says Brown. "And it can be incredibly blasted by storms and rain and winds. So it couldn't be a frail construction. It had to be something very substantial."

The substantiality of the design is marked at the entry, where a six-ton stone column excavated from the site supports a brick-lined, tile-vaulted portico. This entrance connects the house's dark facade to a bright interior. "We have a black exterior, which is the one that fits in with the environment," Brown explains, "but then on the inside we wanted to reflect and bounce the light and create a completely different atmosphere. So when you walk in, there is this complete transformation." The interior uses a white brick from the same Italian manufacturer.

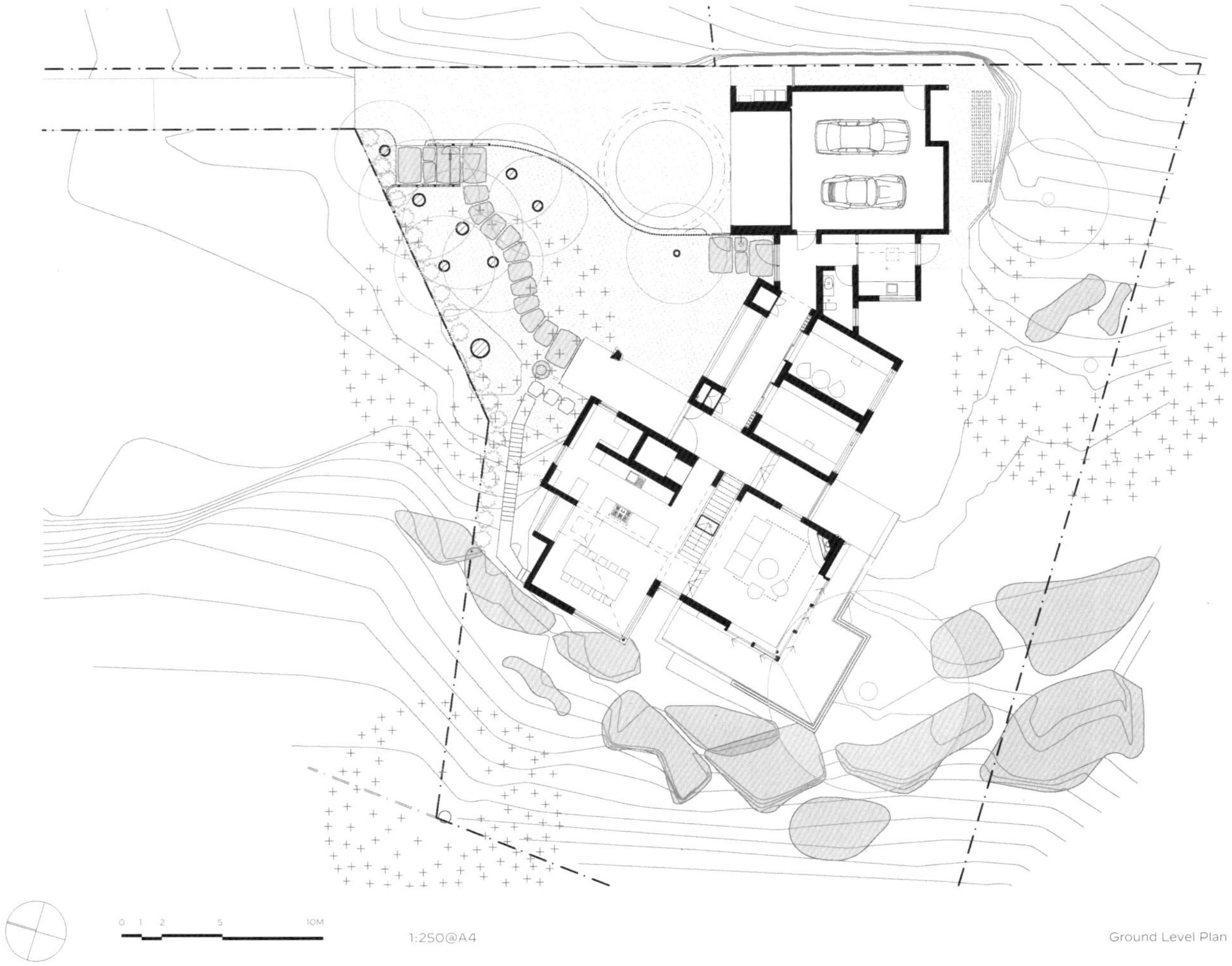

Ground Level Plan

The vaulted entry marks one axis of Bangalley House and leads to panoramic ocean views. "You see whales," says Brown. "You're so high up you see right down onto the beach. You get to see all the surfers. There's fish. It's a panoramic view on all scales." A cross axis runs west from the garage. Along these two axes, slightly more red brick is included in the exterior mix to reflect the red veins that run through the cliff.

To describe the design in plan is to miss its complexity. "The house is made up of small modules that step and stagger down the hill, allowing views and terraces," says Brown, "and that breaking down produces shadows as the sun moves around the building and helps to modulate it." He compares this modulation to European hill villages in Greece, Italy, and Spain.

R
White interior brick reflects light and creates different atmosphere

Bangalley House is conceived as five pavilions set on three levels: bedroom and bath at the top; studies, kitchen, dining, and living rooms in the middle; and guest rooms on the lower level. A central staircase connects the three floors. A sculptural brass screen, designed by Casey Brown Architecture cofounder Caroline Casey, lines the stair. It is meant to be both unnoticed and noticed. "Obviously, when you're looking to the view you don't want that blocked out," says Brown, "but whatever you look at wants to be contributing in a beautiful way to the overall aesthetics of the house." Brass and copper detailing, stone floors, and timber ceilings, along with the white brick, complete the home's minimal, sturdy, interior palette.

After Bangalley House—Casey Brown Architecture's first use of brick in thirty-five years—will the firm build in brick again? "We are building our second one at the moment," says Brown. "Again, one shouldn't be limited by a predisposition to use certain materials in the right circumstances."

TL
Brass and copper detailing, stone floors, timber ceilings, and white brick make up interior palette

—

BL
Sculptural brass screen lines stair

—

R
House is made of small modules that step down hill

JOLYN PLACE

ROSEBERY, NEW SOUTH WALES
AUSTRALIA

BVN ARCHITECTURE

"Jolyn Place responds to the light industrial context that exists at the moment and the future context, which is a lot of much taller, residential, tower-type buildings, some of which already exist in the area."

In designing Jolyn Place, BVN Architecture considered both its past and future home. The competition-winning design is in Green Square, a 687-acre urban renewal area for 61,000 people located 2.5 miles south of Sydney's central business district. "Jolyn Place responds to the light industrial context that exists at the moment," says Matthew Blair, principal of BVN, "and the future context, which is a lot of much taller, residential, tower-type buildings, some of which already exist in the area."

BVN responded to the site with a rectangular building around a central courtyard. Though this is a somewhat standard plan, it is not as basic as it sounds. "The building fills an entire city block and has a publicly accessible central courtyard over two levels, which is quite unusual in Sydney," says Blair. The lower level contains retail space and the upper level a garden. "Usually, these courtyard spaces are secure from the public," says Blair, "but because we have a significant amount of retail space at ground level, it's an active type of development."

Jolyn Place's courtyard—one of more than forty parks and public spaces planned for Green Square—is activated through openings on all four edges of the building. The smaller of the two public connections runs east–west through the site. It enables the public to pass through and not have to walk around the building. The major axis runs north–south through Jolyn Place, linking a large park on the south to a major new urban thoroughfare that is a significant part of Green Square's master plan. "The break in the southern wall of the building is a strong representation of that link," says Blair. "When you see it from the park on the southern side, it really does talk about that connection to the city."

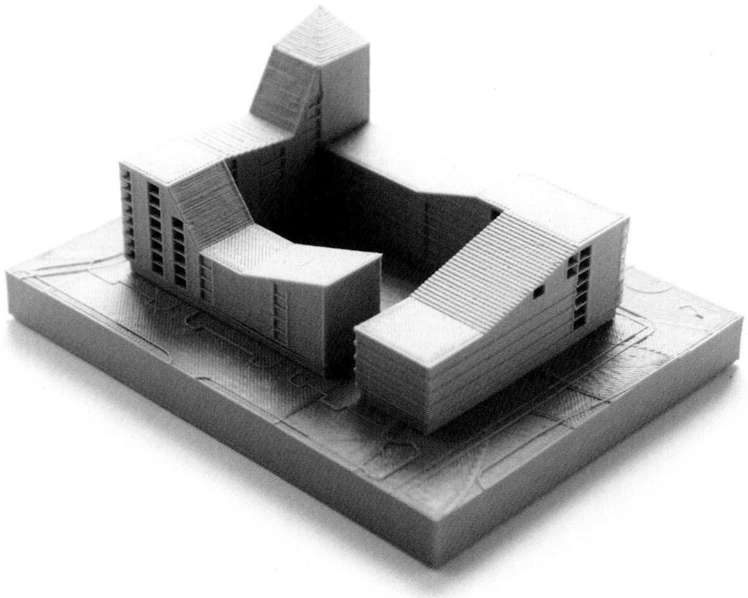

The atypical plan is complemented by an irregular elevation. Jolyn Place's rising and falling roofline responds to views; a tower in the northwest corner overlooks Green Square's town center and offers views to downtown Sydney. The roofline orchestrates sunlight coming into the apartments and the courtyard. And it reacts to both existing and potential neighbors—a roofline meant to represent neither industrial building nor residential tower, but a bit of both. The resulting rich roofscape allows for a many-leveled, planted roof garden, which offers both privacy and a sense of shared community to residents.

Blair says BVN also used the roof design to develop a sense of variety and differentiation across the block without resorting to material changes. BVN wanted to use just one material, brick. They chose San Selmo Smoked brick in three tones—mid-grey, light grey, and black—for all exterior walls, soffits, and passageways. "We spent a significant amount of time experimenting with the color of bricks and mortar," says Blair. Experiments included adjusting the mix through a series of parametric scripts, building test panels on site, and using another project as a prototype of sorts. The architects were looking for a combination in which the bricks had enough similarity that they would offer a monolithic, permanent sense from a distance, provide articulation of the facade upon closer look, and have a recognizable variation in color when viewed up close.

L
Massing model shows complex elevations of building

—

R
All-brick facade stands out from look-at-me neighbors in Green Square

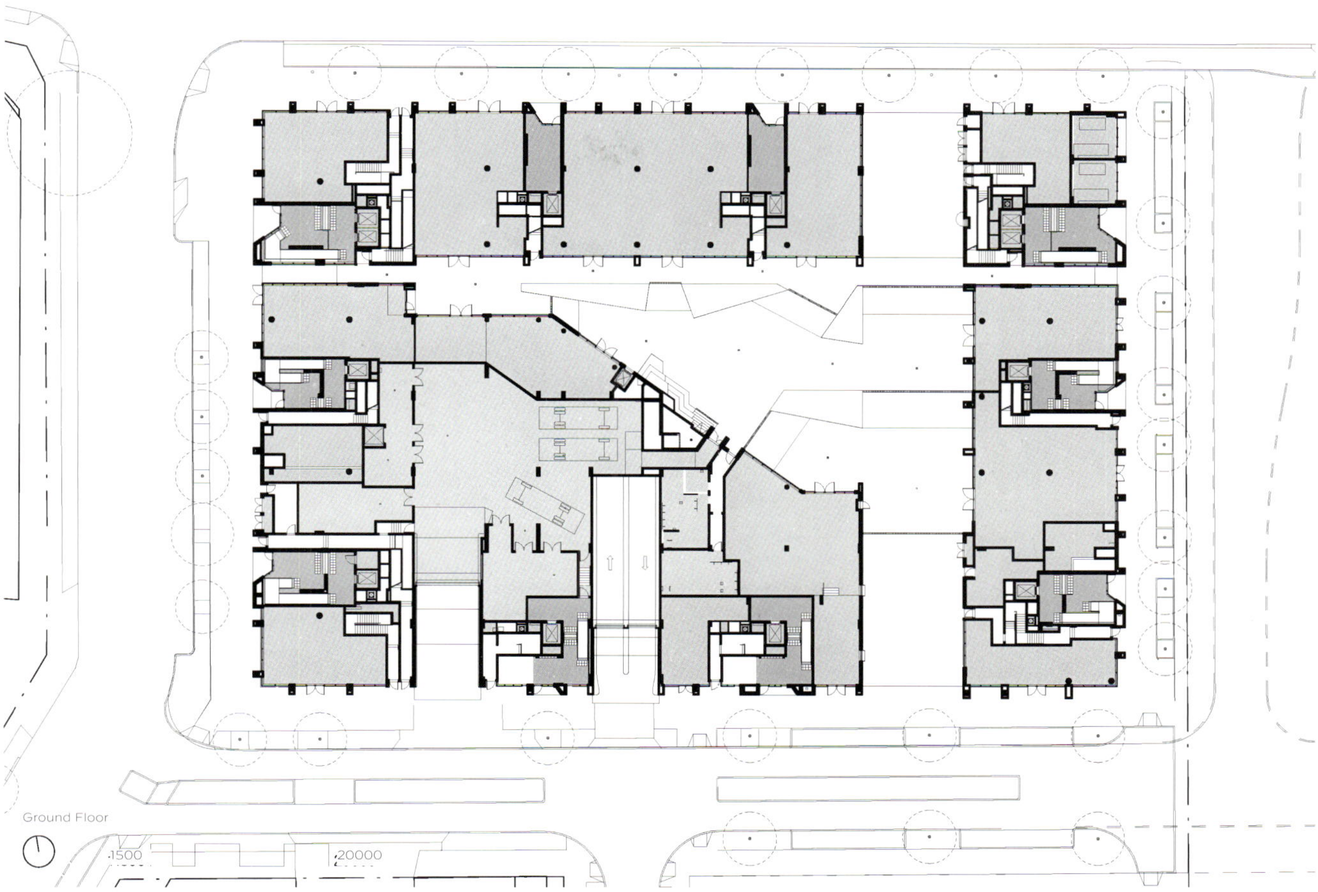

TR
Ground floor plan showing major and minor axes through site

—

BR
Individual residential units are articulated on facade

According to Blair, it took some convincing to get approval to build out of brick alone, as local authorities wanted more variety in new buildings. "Green Square is a little bit of an architectural playground because of its rapid development," he says. He notes that other projects attempt to claim attention with eye-catching angles, projections, colors, and materials. "This building is a quite purposeful rejection of that idea."

L
Lower level of two-story, publicly accessible, central courtyard

L
Photo and rendering
of building viewed
from southeast corner

TR
Many-leveled, planted roof garden offers both privacy and sense of shared community to residents

—

BR
Three tones of brick—mid-grey, light grey, and black—bring variety to exterior

SMART DESIGN STUDIO
ALEXANDRIA, NEW SOUTH WALES
AUSTRALIA

SMART DESIGN STUDIO

"We try to think about the mood that we're trying to create. The mood for living is quite different from the mood for working."

In making a new home for his office and himself, William Smart used brick to promote sustainability, define program types, and allow experimentation. Smart, the creative director of Smart Design Studio, says, "Our philosophy on sustainability is reuse what you can." Converting an old brick shop that manufactured candy machines into the Smart Design Studio met that credo.

The project is located in Alexandria, a suburb of Sydney, in a neighborhood preserved as a conservation area. "It's a really bricky kind of area through here," says Smart. Light industrial shops including an upholsterer, an auto repair shop, and a perfume packager line the streets, along with newer neighbors: a coffee shop, health-food store, and ax-throwing venue. Smart sought to design a new version of an industrial building, one that uses "everyday, robust, ordinary, inexpensive materials." These include rope for outdoor furniture, galvanized steel for roofs, tiles for flooring, wire for stair supports, and brick for walls.

The shop's original brick walls, cleaned up and reset with steel-framed windows, form the rear of the new studio. Painted white on the inside, the walls enclose a large, open-plan work area converted from two sheds. (A third renovated shed is separated by a new brick wall and leased out.) The studio maintains its original sawtooth roof and south-facing clerestory windows, which provide favorable soft light. Natural ventilation and radiant floor heating and cooling add to Smart Design Studio's sustainable design.

The front of the old building, which had included a hodgepodge of additions, was not a good candidate for renovation. So Smart Design Studio replaced it with a three-story addition whose brick facade serves as an advertisement of sorts for the firm's design work. An awning of specialty curved bricks provides cover at the entrance and distinguishes the building from its boxy industrial neighbors. Smart's idea for the curves is that the brick wall peels open to windows and doors. "Just walking down the street," he says, "it presents as quite sculptural."

TL
Front elevation and transverse section

—

BL
Ground floor, second floor, and third floor plans

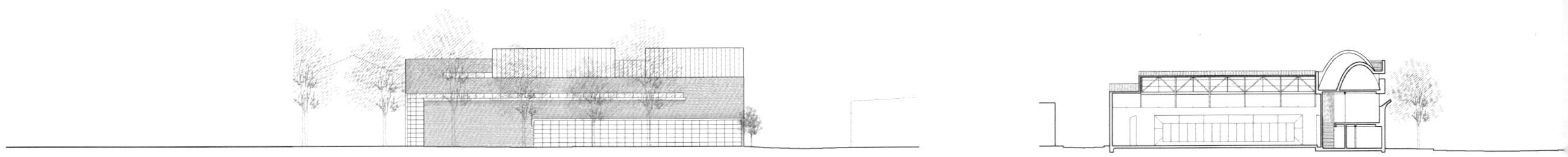

Behind this facade are ground-floor reception, second-floor break rooms, and a third-floor caretaker residence. Smart and his partner are, appropriately, the caretakers keeping watch on the building. The curve-filled design of the residence is dramatically different from that of the orthogonal office below. Smart says it responds to his studio's philosophy of designing architecture from the inside out. "We try to think about the mood that we're trying to create," he says. "The mood for living is quite different from the mood for working."

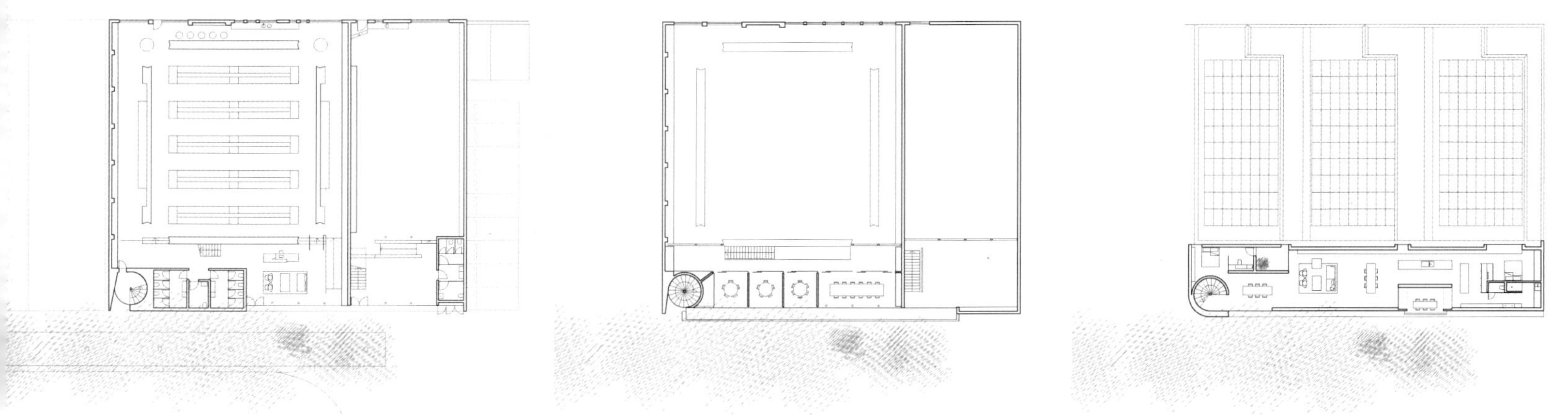

R
New brick facade on old building serves as advertisement of architects' design work

L
Brick wall peels open to windows and doors

—

TR
New design studio in old sawtooth-roofed space

—

BR
Work spaces and break rooms surround the open office

L
Caretaker residence with brick catenary arch

The residential mood is enhanced by a series of brick catenary arches that define areas within the open plan. The catenary, a shape that mimics the drape of a chain turned upside down, has long been popular in architecture, from the dome of Christopher Wren's St. Paul's Cathedral to the interior of Antoni Gaudí's La Sagrada Familia to the entirety of Eero Saarinen's Gateway Arch. Smart chose the catenary for "the purity of it." In addition, the architect was attracted to its durability. "If you were to make, say, a barrel vault with two vertical walls and a round top," he explains, "over time, especially with brick, it would just slightly lean out. In theory, this perfect shape will not change over time." Even a small lean could affect the work, as glass is set within the brick arch. Longevity is important to Smart. "This is our forever home, we hope," he says.

Another reason behind the catenary was an opportunity for experimentation—to try something Smart Design Studio had not done before. The architects brought in a university-based parametrics expert to assist with the design, and they built and tested a full-scale prototype before building it on site. The bricks were laid without mortar. They were set atop plywood shells and glued together with a terra-cotta tile glue. Using the firm itself as the guinea pig allowed for this experimentation, and the arches now serve as exemplars of the studio's capabilities.

TR
Glass intersects with arch to bring light into space

—

BR
Full-scale prototype of arch was desigend and tested before building on site

ORO EDITIONS
PUBLISHERS OF ARCHITECTURE, ART, AND DESIGN
Publisher: Gordon Goff

www.oroeditions.com
info@oroeditions.com

Published by ORO Editions

Author and Project Editor: Clare Jacobson
Designer: Connie Hwang Design
Managing Editor: Jake Anderson

10 9 8 7 6 5 4 3 2 1
First Edition

ISBN: 978-1-957183-20-6

Color Separations and Printing: ORO Group Ltd. Printed in China.

ORO Editions makes a continuous effort to minimize the overall carbon footprint of its publications. As part of this goal, ORO Editions, in association with Global ReLeaf, arranges to plant trees to replace those used in the manufacturing of the paper produced for its books. Global ReLeaf is an international campaign run by American Forests, one of the world's oldest nonprofit conservation organizations. Global ReLeaf is American Forests' education and action program that helps individuals, organizations, agencies, and corporations improve the local and global environment by planting and caring for trees.

Cover: 45 East 7th Street, Morris Adjmi Architects, photo © Donna Chiarelli
ii: Smart Design Studio, Smart Design Studio, photo Romello Pereira
iv: Nicholas S. Zeppos College, Vanderbilt University, David M. Schwarz Architects, photo Steve Hall, Hall+Hendrick+McCaugherty Photographers
vi: Jolyn Place, BVN Architecture, photo Katherine Lu for BVN Architecture
2: 45 East 7th Street, Morris Adjmi Architects, photo © Donna Chiarelli

All images © Donna Chiarelli except for the following:
7T, 8, 11, 14, 21B: Morris Adjmi Architects
15L: Jimi Billingsley
15R: Nexus Development
16–17: Selvon Ramsawak
21T: Williams New York
24: Substance Architecture
25, 27: Corey Gaffer
30, 32T, 33: Stephen B. Jacobs Group, Architects and Planners
34, 35: Ben Fitchett
38: David Sparks Photography
39T, 41: TowerPinkster
44, 48, 49T: Peter VanderPoel
50–51, 52, 54B, 55–57: Steve Hall, Hall+Hendrick+McCaugherty Photographers
54T: David M. Schwarz Architects
58, 60T, 61, 62, 63B, 64, 65: Kevin Belanger
60B, 63T: Mateusz Nowacki, Everyday Studio
66–68, 71–73: Michael Nicholson
70: Casey Brown Architecture
74, 78, 80T: Barton Taylor for BVN Architecture
76, 79T, 80B: BVN Architecture
77, 79B: Martin Siegner
81: Katherine Lu for BVN Architecture
82, 85–89: Romello Pereira
84: Smart Design Studio